The Foolishness of God, the Hidden Wisdom, and the Mind of Christ

30 Lessons from 1 Corinthians 1-4

Joshua Nickel

The Foolishness of God, the Hidden Wisdom, and the Mind of Christ: 30 Lessons from 1 Corinthians 1-4

Contents

30 Lessons from 1 Corinthians 1-4

Introduction

In 1 Corinthians 1:18, the apostle Paul called his gospel *"the message of the cross."* This was the message that he had preached and lived by when he had first come to Corinth.

There was a problem, however. The Corinthians had already heard a message of the cross, as preached by the Roman Empire.

The cross already had a message before Paul ever came to Corinth. Before Jesus was ever crucified, the cross was being used by the Roman Empire to speak its own word.

Crucifixion was not the most efficient way to execute a criminal. It was used because it sent an unforgettable message. It communicated shame, defeat, weakness, and humiliation in the most visceral and immediate way the Romans could find.

"If you defy the Roman Empire you will lose." The Romans wanted this to be clear and unmistakable, and nothing said "loser" any louder or faster than a crucifixion did. The Romans got their message across, and everyone took it to heart—almost everyone, that is.

We are told in Hebrews 12:2 that Jesus *despised* the shame of the cross. That means He scorned, ignored, and thought nothing of it. He understood the shame that the cross was meant to evoke, but He didn't take it seriously. He blew it off.

Paul, likewise, was unintimidated and unashamed. He knew what the cross of the world was supposed to say, but the cross of Christ had said something much more important, and it had said it with much greater authority.

Fortunately for the Corinthians, and for us, Paul took the time to explain, in 1 Corinthians 1-4, what his "message of the cross" looked like in real life.

This book consists of thirty lessons taken from 1 Corinthians 1-4, sometimes looking at several verses at once, sometimes looking at just one verse or less. These lessons are not based exclusively on what is said in the first four chapters of 1 Corinthians, but draw from other parts of the Bible as well.

These lessons can each stand alone and can thus be read out of order, but I hope that reading them in order will also give you a sense of the progress of Paul's argument in 1 Corinthians 1-4.

Above all, I hope that this book will deepen your appreciation for a great passage of the Bible and for the message of the gospel. If you have resolved to proclaim, in word and in deed, by your life and by your example, the message of Jesus Christ and Him crucified, then it would be an honor if this book can serve you in any way. I hope it brings edification and encouragement to the people marked by the cross.

Lesson #1:

Those Who Ignore Their Cultural Biases Are Bound to Be Influenced by Them

Paul, called to be an apostle of Jesus Christ through the will of God, and Sosthenes our brother,

To the church of God which is at Corinth, to those who are sanctified in Christ Jesus, called to be saints, with all who in every place call on the name of Jesus Christ our Lord, both theirs and ours:

Grace to you and peace from God our Father and the Lord Jesus Christ.

I thank my God always concerning you for the grace of God which was given to you by Christ Jesus, that you were enriched in everything by Him in all utterance and all knowledge, even as the testimony of Christ was confirmed in you, so that you come short in no gift, eagerly waiting for the revelation of our Lord Jesus Christ, who will also confirm you to the end, that you may be blameless in the day of our Lord Jesus Christ. God is faithful, by whom you were called into the fellowship of His Son, Jesus Christ our Lord.

1 Corinthians 1:1-9

Paul opens this letter with a greeting that is similar to the ones in his other letters. There are, however, little differences. These differences are hints about issues that he is going to be dealing with.

For example, he addresses the Corinthians as, *"those who are sanctified in Christ Jesus, called to be saints."* They needed to be reminded of their sanctification, and here, in the first sentence, is a double reminder. Much of the Corinthians' behavior was far from holy, and needed to be corrected. They were living in conflict with the sanctifying work of God in their lives.

Another hint at an issue that needed to be dealt with is found in this line: *"...with all who in every place call on the name of Jesus Christ our Lord, both theirs and ours."* This is a reminder that they were not the only believers in the world, and that the gospel did not begin and end with them.

The Corinthians had received many gifts from God, including much revelation and knowledge. This was a point of pride for them, as if it set them apart and made them a special church.

Sometimes we still think this way today, and when we do, we are just as wrong as the Corinthians were. In reality, spiritual revelation does not set us apart from the rest of the body of Christ. It establishes us within the body.

Consider Paul's prayer for another church to receive spiritual revelation. This prayer is found in Ephesians 3:14-21:

For this reason I bow my knees to the Father of our Lord Jesus Christ, from whom the whole family in heaven and earth is named, that He would grant you, according to the riches of His glory, to be strengthened with might through His Spirit in the inner man, that Christ may dwell in your hearts through faith; that you, being rooted and grounded in love, may be able to comprehend with all the saints what is the width and length and depth and height— to know the love of Christ which passes knowledge; that you may be filled with all the fullness of God.

Now to Him who is able to do exceedingly abundantly above all that we ask or think, according to the power that works in us, to Him be glory in the church by Christ Jesus to all generations, forever and ever. Amen.

There are three things that Paul says in this prayer that remind us that spiritual revelation is given to us as we appreciate our fellow believers, and that it is given to deepen that appreciation.

First: *"the whole family in heaven and earth."* Paul prayed with an awareness of his fellow saints alive at that time as well as those who had gone before him.

Second: *"to comprehend with all the saints."* The revelation of the glory of God is our common heritage.

Third: *"to Him be glory in the church by Christ Jesus to all generations, forever and ever."* Although Paul's letters sometimes reveal an expectation that Jesus would return soon, he really did not know how soon it would happen. Here he remains mindful of the future generations, however many there may be. They will also share in the revelation of the glory of Christ.

So spiritual revelation should create within us a greater awareness of our spiritual heritage, and a humble thankfulness to be part of such a great family, past, present, and possibly future.

The Corinthians, however, were puffed up by the very knowledge that was supposed keep them humble. Before they had heard the gospel, they were already proud of their culture, and what they thought it meant to be Corinthian. They brought that pride with them into their Christian experience.

Before Paul wrote 1 Corinthians, he wrote 1 and 2 Thessalonians. In those letters, he addressed the church like this: *"to the church of the Thessalonians in God the Father and the Lord Jesus Christ."*

That's a fine way to address the churches in Thessalonica, but it wouldn't do for the Corinthians. Their concept of Christianity was already too Corinthian. They were well aware of the Corinthian nature of their church, and proud of it. The emphasis needed to go elsewhere.

Paul did not address them as the "the church of the Corinthians" but as "the church *of God* which is *at Corinth."*

The Corinthians needed to broaden their horizon. They were making the same mistake we all make to some degree: they assumed that their cultural values were universal, or at least better than other cultures' values.

In reality, all cultures have some values and traditions that the church can use and some that the church must reject. These things do not sort themselves out automatically, however. The church must exercise discernment in accepting some traditions and rejecting others. Work is required, and the Corinthians had not done the work.

Sometimes people claim they are not following any traditions of men at all, but only following what the Bible says. That's a fine thing to say, but if they don't examine the traditions of their own culture, they will follow them by default. Often, when someone says, "I don't follow traditions, I only follow what the Bible says," what they're really saying is, "I don't even know what traditions I'm following."

Such people are like the group in Corinth that we will encounter in our next lesson, those who were dividing from the rest of the church while saying, "I am of Christ." If they had really been of Christ they would not have been competitive and divisive. Their intention was noble, but they were not really doing what they said. (At least those who said, "I am of Paul," or "I am of Apollos" admitted that they were choosing sides.)

Actually *being* "of Christ" in relation to the rest of the church is not as easy as saying that you are. Likewise, following the Bible instead the traditions of men is not as easy as it sounds. It requires that we be aware of the traditions that influence us, rejecting some and keeping others.

When we understand our own culture, we can not only reject was is unbiblical, but we can hold onto what is good. Philippians 4:8 can help us to do this work. It gives us a good list of criteria to help decide what to promote about a culture:

"Finally, brethren, whatever things are true, whatever things are noble, whatever things are just, whatever things are pure, whatever things are lovely, whatever things are of good report, if there is any virtue and if there is anything praiseworthy—meditate on these things."

There are many forces in this world trying to influence our thinking. We have been given the privilege and responsibility of freedom. This does not mean that we are free from all outside influence, but that we can choose what we allow to influence us.

Lesson #1: Those Who Ignore Their Cultural Biases Are Bound to Be Influenced by Them

Lesson #2:

The Goal of a Servant of God Is to Disappear (the Hard Way, Not the Easy Way)

Now I plead with you, brethren, by the name of our Lord Jesus Christ, that you all speak the same thing, and that there be no divisions among you, but that you be perfectly joined together in the same mind and in the same judgment. For it has been declared to me concerning you, my brethren, by those of Chloe's household, that there are contentions among you. Now I say this, that each of you says, "I am of Paul," or "I am of Apollos," or "I am of Cephas," or "I am of Christ."

1 Corinthians 1:10-12

Genesis 5:24 tells us about Enoch, who *"walked with God; and he was not, for God took him."*

The name *Enoch* means *teacher* or *teaching,* and Enoch was a great teacher to us all. Although the Bible doesn't give us many of his words, the greatest lesson he taught was his walk with God.

The book of Genesis also tells us about another Enoch. This Enoch was Adam's grandson, so he was born a bit earlier than the one who walked with God, and this one probably did not walk with God. He was the son of Cain, who was history's first murderer.

This earlier Enoch is not as well-known today, but in those days, he was probably more famous than the other Enoch. The first city ever built was named after him.

Genesis 4:16-17 tells the story: *"Then Cain went out from the presence of the Lord and dwelt in the land of Nod on the east of Eden. And Cain knew his wife, and she conceived and bore Enoch. And he built a city, and called the name of the city after the name of his son—Enoch."*

A person's name meant something in those days. These two men were probably named *Enoch* because they were intended to teach humanity something. They taught very different lessons, however.

The first Enoch taught the ways of the world. The city that bore his name represented his father Cain's attempt to establish security for himself without the need for God.

The second Enoch taught the opposite lesson. For he walked with God, and everyone who walks with God finds that their need for Him—their utter dependence upon Him—only increases with time.

When the first Enoch died, he left behind a city named after him. No doubt he was remembered for generations. The second Enoch did not even leave his own body behind. Yet it is he who has been remembered longer, and who is still teaching us today.

The apostle Paul followed the example of the second Enoch in his ministry, always pointing past himself, to God. He summed up his approach to ministry in 2 Corinthians 4:5: *"For we do not preach ourselves, but Christ Jesus the Lord."*

There were ministers in Paul's day who *did* preach themselves, and they used the name of Christ to draw men to themselves. They stirred up division. We can see their influence when we read 2 Corinthians 10-13, where Paul had to clean up the mess they made.

But Paul wasn't like that. Certainly Peter (whom Paul, in his letters, called Cephas) wasn't like that either. Apollos was also a sincere minister of Christ, otherwise Paul would not have urged him to visit the Corinthians again (see 1 Corinthians 16:12).

So how were the Corinthians so easily divided under the banners of these ministers' names? Couldn't these great men of God have done more to prevent this? Did they perhaps preach themselves instead of Christ, at least a little bit?

No, it's not their fault, but yes, they did preach themselves. They had no choice.

Look again at the verse I shared above: *"For we do not preach ourselves, but Christ Jesus the Lord."*

That's not the full verse. It's only half a sentence, and it doesn't fully represent Paul's model of ministry. 2 Corinthians 4:5 actually says this: *"For we do not preach ourselves, but Christ Jesus the Lord, and ourselves your bondservants for Jesus' sake."*

Paul, Peter, and Apollos could not hide behind the gospel. They had to give themselves to the people along with the gospel they proclaimed. This is the sense in which they preached themselves—as servants for Jesus' sake.

Look at Paul's letters. He talks a lot about Jesus Christ, but the first word in all of his letters is *Paul.*

Servants in those days were often overlooked or under-appreciated, but they were not anonymous. I imagine that sometimes Paul wished he *could* remain anonymous. That would have been easier.

The easy way is to hide behind the gospel, as if you were no more responsible for your own words than Balaam's donkey was for his (see Numbers 2).

The hard way is to give yourself to the people you serve, but to walk so close to God that you are getting out of the way even as you are giving yourself away. That's the way of Enoch, and of Paul, Peter, and Apollos. That's the way that we are all called to live out our lives.

Lesson #2: The Goal of a Servant of God Is to Disappear (the Hard Way, Not the Easy Way)

Lesson #3:

The Temptation to Envy Must Not Just Be Resisted, but Strategically Pre-empted

Is Christ divided? Was Paul crucified for you? Or were you baptized in the name of Paul?

I thank God that I baptized none of you except Crispus and Gaius, lest anyone should say that I had baptized in my own name. Yes, I also baptized the household of Stephanas. Besides, I do not know whether I baptized any other. For Christ did not send me to baptize, but to preach the gospel, not with wisdom of words, lest the cross of Christ should be made of no effect.

1 Corinthians 1:13-17

How is it that Paul could have baptized so few people? He certainly appreciated the value of baptism (see, for example, Romans 6 and Colossians 2).

It appears, from 1 Corinthians 1:13-17, that Paul made a conscious effort not to baptize people unless there was nobody else to do it.

If this is indeed the case, then there is a good reason why he would have done that: to prevent the kind of rivalries that the Corinthians were experiencing. If

Paul had baptized people himself, it would have given them more to argue about: who was baptized by who, and which minister baptized more people.

It would not have been the first time that baptism was viewed as a competition. We can see it beginning to happen in the days of John the Baptist and Jesus.

All four Gospels chronicle how the opponents of Jesus harassed and persecuted Him. His public ministry had barely begun before there were scribes from Jerusalem everywhere He went, trying to catch Him in His words and bring Him down.

John 3:22-27 reports something that happened early in Jesus' ministry, before John the Baptist had been arrested. Certain Jews came to John the Baptist with some interesting news about Jesus:

After these things Jesus and His disciples came into the land of Judea, and there He remained with them and baptized. Now John also was baptizing in Aenon near Salim, because there was much water there. And they came and were baptized. For John had not yet been thrown into prison.

Then there arose a dispute between some of John's disciples and the Jews about purification. And they came to John and said to him, "Rabbi, He who was with you beyond the Jordan, to whom you have testified—behold, He is baptizing, and all are coming to Him!"

This seemingly harmless statement was actually the beginning of the persecution against Jesus that would eventually lead to His crucifixion. It was meant to make John the Baptist jealous. The enemies of Jesus knew that they could bring Him down without lifting a finger if they could stir up rivalry between Jesus and John, or at least between their disciples.

Jesus saw this strategy for what it was, as John 4:1-3 indicates:

Therefore, when the Lord knew that the Pharisees had heard that Jesus made and baptized more disciples than John (though Jesus Himself did not baptize, but His disciples), He left Judea and departed again to Galilee.

The strategy failed that time, but it doesn't always fail. Unfortunately, it's often very effective. That's why the enemy of the gospel still uses it today against God's servants.

And just as it was in those days, it is often the enemy's first line of attack today. This is because it is efficient. A small seed of envy, unless it is uprooted, can grow into a spirit of rivalry and competition that sidetracks the work of the gospel.

Jesus invested a lot of time in teaching twelve men to avoid this trap, as we see when we read the Gospels. This investment paid off, as we see when we read Acts.

John the Baptist was also too smart to fall for this trick. He was too aware of his own calling and purpose. His answer to this challenge set the standard for all future ministers of the gospel: *"He must increase,"* John said, *"but I must decrease"* (John 3:30).

As we saw in the previous lesson, this is the way of Enoch: to decrease into the greatness of God. Enoch did this so well that he literally disappeared. John the Baptist did it too, in his own way. All of God's servants are called to do this in one way or another.

But it's not really something you can do. It's something that happens to you as you walk with God. It's something only God can do.

John the Baptist's words also demonstrate this. When he says of Christ, *"He must increase,"* he is using an active verb. Increasing is something that Christ does. When John says, *"I must decrease,"* he is using a passive verb. This is something being done to him. He is really saying, "I must be decreased."

The greatness of Jesus Christ does this to a person. Jesus said that His disciples would lose their lives for His sake. Although many of them would eventually be killed because of the gospel, Jesus was describing not just those martyrs, but all His future disciples.

To lose your life in this way is to find it. To be decreased before God is not to come to nothing. On the contrary, it is to come to God. It is to come to everything.

As we will see further on in our study, it is those who refuse this way who will be brought to nothing, even as they try to make themselves into something.

Lesson #3: The Temptation to Envy Must Not Just Be Resisted, but Strategically Pre-empted

Lesson #4:

The Message of the Cross Is Both Foolishness and Power, or It's Not the Message of the Cross

For the message of the cross is foolishness to those who are perishing, but to us who are being saved it is the power of God. For it is written:

"I will destroy the wisdom of the wise, And bring to nothing the understanding of the prudent."

1 Corinthians 1:18-19

The passage Paul quotes here is Isaiah 29:14. Paul quoted Isaiah often in his letters, about forty times.

Jesus also quoted the book of Isaiah often, and declared that He was fulfilling it. Luke 4:16-21 is a good example of this. It tells us that Jesus went into a synagogue, read a passage from Isaiah that had been traditionally understood as describing the coming Christ, and said, *"Today this Scripture is fulfilled in your hearing."* That's straightforward enough for anyone who was paying attention.

When an imprisoned John the Baptist sent messengers to Jesus, asking if He was the One they had been waiting for, He told them, *"Go and tell John the things which you hear and see: The blind see and the lame walk; the lepers are cleansed and the deaf hear; the dead are raised up and the poor have the gospel preached to them."* (Matthew 11:4-5)

Jesus was doing the things the prophets said the Christ would do and saying the things the prophets said the Christ would say. Still, people doubted if He was the Christ.

Imagine you are an actor or an actress in a play, and you are the only one who has memorized their lines—in fact, you're the only one who has even read the script! This was Jesus' situation, except in His case, everyone else *had* read the script (Isaiah and the rest of the Old Testament), they just didn't understand it.

One time when the Pharisees were harassing Jesus about something, He told them that they were acting just as Isaiah had prophesied:

"Hypocrites! Well did Isaiah prophesy about you, saying:

'These people draw near to Me with their mouth,
And honor Me with their lips,
But their heart is far from Me.
And in vain they worship Me,
Teaching as doctrines the commandments of men.'"

(Matthew 15:7-9)

Jesus quoted Isaiah 29:13 that day. If anyone who was listening had access to a copy of Isaiah, they could have gone and looked it up. In fact, they should have, because Jesus was letting them know where they were in the script and what scene was coming next.

If someone had gone and read the verse that Jesus had quoted to them along with the very next verse, they would have seen this:

"Therefore the Lord said:

'Inasmuch as these people draw near with their mouths
And honor Me with their lips,
But have removed their hearts far from Me,
And their fear toward Me is taught by the commandment of
men,
Therefore, behold, I will again do a marvelous work
Among this people,
A marvelous work and a wonder;
For the wisdom of their wise men shall perish,
And the understanding of their prudent men shall be hidden.'"

(Isaiah 29:13-14)

"A marvelous work!" This is what God was saying through Isaiah and in Jesus: "A marvelous work and a wonder is going to happen, and you don't have to miss it. You can be a part of it. All you have to know is that you know nothing. You know nothing and the smartest person among you knows nothing and this work that I am going to do among you is going to prove it."

Of course, nobody saw the marvelous work coming until after it was accomplished. But even after it was fulfilled by God and proclaimed by the apostles, some people continued to miss it. The message of the cross was foolishness to some even as it was power to others.

So much has changed in the two thousand years since Paul wrote 1 Corinthians. The gospel has been proclaimed to every kind of culture and society on earth, in times of war and times of peace. Yet despite all that has changed, Paul's description of the message of the cross remains remarkably accurate. It's still foolishness and it's still power.

Paul was faced with a choice. He could have tried to mitigate the foolishness of the message by his own cleverness, but to do so would have been to remove its power. He decided ahead of time that he wasn't going to do that. He counted the cost and preached a foolish message that he knew would bring ridicule and persecution, and he preached it with power.

Paul bore witness to the power of God at work in his generation. Christians today may be tempted to wonder, "Where is the power of God in *this* generation?"

Perhaps every generation has asked that question. Throughout church history there have always been those who read the New Testament, looked at the church, and were profoundly disappointed by the comparison.

Fortunately, not everybody stopped there. In every generation there have been those who found the power. And they always found it in the same place.

The power has never left. It has been in the same place all along. It is the message the cross. Jesus crucified for sinners is the power of God, and it has been the power of God for two thousand years.

But it is also foolishness, and it has been foolishness for two thousand years. You can't have the power without the foolishness.

It is fair to ask, "Where is the power of God in this generation?" But a better question is, "Where are the fools?"

I don't mean those who are fools in the eyes of God. Those kinds of fools are easy to find. They are everywhere. But where are those who have embraced the message of the cross without qualification or reservation? Find those fools, and you will find the power of God.

As I said, Paul counted the cost, made a decision, and stuck with it. But it was also a daily decision, because it was tested daily. That's why his teaching in 1 Corinthians 1-4 is so helpful to every Christian. We all go through the same temptations. We all fall short. Paul wrote not to shame but to teach. There is hope for all of us who are still tempted by the desire to appear wise and powerful in this world.

1 Corinthians 1-4 helps us to avoid the traps of worldly thinking. And our world is the same one that Paul and the Corinthians lived in, despite all the superficial changes. It is fundamentally the same place it has always been. The world doesn't change because human nature doesn't change. There is nothing being

written today that is going to be more relevant to a disciple of Jesus Christ than 1 Corinthians 1-4 is.

Lesson #4: The Message of the Cross Is Both Foolishness and Power, or It's Not the Message of the Cross

Lesson #5:

Until We See the Wisdom of God's Foolishness and the Foolishness of Our Wisdom, We Haven't Encountered the Power of the Cross

Where is the wise? Where is the scribe? Where is the disputer of this age? Has not God made foolish the wisdom of this world? For since, in the wisdom of God, the world through wisdom did not know God, it pleased God through the foolishness of the message preached to save those who believe.

1 Corinthians 1:20-21

God can't be reached by our own efforts. He can't be known by our wisdom and He can't be impressed by our morality. In fact, nothing impresses God. What could? Even a philosopher of this age, reasoning with human wisdom, could reach the conclusion that God is not impressed by anything we do.

What that philosopher could not know, however, is whether or not God could ever be pleased, and what that pleasure might look like. This is what the gospel reveals: not what impresses God, but what pleases Him.

God is pleased to save us. He saves us from self-deception and self-destruction, and He saves us from our own efforts—even our efforts at knowing and understanding Him.

Once saved by God's foolishness, however, we can then apply our minds to knowing and understanding Him. The gospel is not anti-intellectual. It encourages vigorous thinking. But all such reasoning must be true to the word of the cross. We cannot choose between wise theology and foolish theology. Our theology will be faithful to the foolishness of God, or it will veer into the foolishness of men. That is our choice.

The Greeks at Corinth valued a certain kind of wisdom and rhetoric. A skilled debater could become a celebrity in Corinth. The Corinthians were so impressed by eloquence and knowledge that they thought of God in these terms, or that these things pointed to God.

This was a mistake. The wisdom of God is not a hyper-exalted version of human wisdom. The same could be said of God's strength. It is not simply human strength infinitely increased. God is not a superman. He is greater than us, but He is also *different* from us. His wisdom and power are not only greater than ours by degrees, but also very different—marked by unapproachable purity and holiness.

Different cultures value different things, but one way or another, all humans make the mistake of understanding God in human terms. We can't help it. We get it from our father.

Adam was made in the image of God. His purpose was to look like God. He was to make known, throughout creation, what God is like. But he abandoned this purpose when he sinned against God. He was no longer fit for the job, and neither are his children, although we still try.

Romans 1:22-23 describes how sin had corrupted mankind: *"Professing to be wise, they became fools, and changed the glory of the incorruptible God into an image made like corruptible man—and birds and four-footed animals and creeping things."*

Humanity had made a mess of things, calling foolishness wisdom, and wisdom foolishness. While we were in this condition, God couldn't come to us in a wisdom that impressed us. That would have just increased our confidence in our own wisdom—wisdom so great that it can even recognize God when it sees Him! Instead, He gave us His wisdom wrapped in foolishness, and His strength wrapped in weakness.

Proverbs 26:4 says, *"Do not answer a fool according to his folly, lest you also be like him."*

You can't reason with a fool by making the same mistakes he's making. If you accept his erroneous assumptions, you're "answering him according to his folly." You will not impart wisdom to him, you will share in his foolishness. If he is building on a foolish foundation, you cannot help him by building on the same foundation.

If you really want to help a fool, destroy his foundation. As a modern-day debater might say, you must reject the premise of his argument.

A gospel that appeals to man on the basis of his own wisdom would leave a fundamental problem unsolved: man's wisdom is foolishness.

(Bear in mind, here, that what Paul refers to in 1 Corinthians as the wisdom of man and the wisdom of the world is not the same thing as simple human intelligence. That's a gift from God, as we will consider in Lesson #24.)

Proverbs 26:4 has been place side by side with another, similar Proverb. Proverbs 26:5 says, *"Answer a fool according to his folly, lest he be wise in his own eyes."*

Here we see that there is another way to "answer a fool according to his folly." This is a way that works, a way that will deliver him from his error. If you can answer a fool in this way, he will see his so-called wisdom for the foolishness that it really is.

So how do you answer a fool in such a way that reveals his foolishness? People might give you various answers about how they do it. What really matters for us here is how God did it: by the word of the cross.

God has answered us. At the cross, our foolishness is exposed. Our religious attempt at making a god in our own image is revealed for what it is: sin.

In the word of the cross, God has rejected our premise. He has destroyed our religious foundation. He has met us where we are and answered us according to our foolishness.

Lesson #5: Until We See the Wisdom of God's Foolishness and the Foolishness of Our Wisdom, We Haven't Encountered the Power of the Cross

Lesson #6:

Until We See the Power of God's Weakness and the Weakness of Our Power, We Haven't Encountered the Wisdom of the Cross

For Jews request a sign, and Greeks seek after wisdom; but we preach Christ crucified, to the Jews a stumbling block and to the Greeks foolishness, but to those who are called, both Jews and Greeks, Christ the power of God and the wisdom of God.

1 Corinthians 1:22-24

As we will see later on in our study, Paul reminds the Corinthians that when he had first come to Corinth, he preached the gospel to them *"in demonstration of the Spirit and of power"* (1 Corinthians 2:4). Here, in the passage quoted above, Paul says, *"Jews request a sign."* If it was just any sign that they wanted, then all the unbelieving Jews in Corinth would have been satisfied by Paul's ministry.

For that matter, the miracles of Jesus should have been enough for the Pharisees. They weren't, however, as we are told in Mark 8:11-12:

"Then the Pharisees came out and began to dispute with Him, seeking from Him a sign from heaven, testing Him. But He sighed deeply in His spirit, and said, 'Why does this generation seek a sign? Assuredly, I say to you, no sign shall be given to this generation.'"

Jesus exercised power over demons and over every kind of disease. He calmed a storm one time and His disciples marveled that even the wind and the sea obeyed Him.

Yet the Pharisees didn't see the sign they were looking for because they didn't see the kind of power they were interested in: power to control people.

Jesus was the Great Shepherd, there's no doubt about it. But He didn't shepherd goats. He said, "My sheep hear my voice." Those who didn't hear what they wanted to hear stopped listening, and He didn't force them to stay.

Even those who were on His side weren't the greatest listeners.

Sometimes, when Jesus healed people, he told them not to tell anyone. There are theories about why He did this. I think it was a matter of crowd control. He wanted to have time to visit all the cities and villages of Galilee, to reach people where they lived. Also, He sometimes withdrew to the wilderness to have time to pray, which the crowds made increasingly difficult.

Regardless of why Jesus told people not to tell anyone about a particular healing, my point is this: it never worked. They didn't listen to Him.

You would think that if a man healed you of a life-threatening disease or raised your daughter from the dead, you would do what He asked, even if it didn't make sense to you at the time.

No. Not once. They always spread the word about Jesus, even when He told them not to. Here's an example of this from Mark 7:32-37:

"Then they brought to Him one who was deaf and had an impediment in his speech, and they begged Him to put His hand on him. And He took him aside from the multitude, and put His fingers in his ears, and He spat and touched his tongue. Then, looking up to heaven, He sighed, and said to him, 'Ephphatha,' that is, 'Be opened.'

"Immediately his ears were opened, and the impediment of his tongue was loosed, and he spoke plainly. Then He commanded them that they should tell no one; but the more He commanded them, the more widely they proclaimed it. And they were astonished beyond measure, saying, 'He has done all things well. He makes both the deaf to hear and the mute to speak'"

They praised Him while disobeying Him: "He has done all thing well! He just can't get us to do what He says."

Jesus' opponents put Him on trial and then challenged Him for not responding to false accusations. While He was being crucified they mocked Him, saying, *"He saved others; Himself He cannot save. Let the*

Christ, the King of Israel, descend now from the cross, that we may see and believe." (Mark 15:31-32)

They were asking for a sign right up to the end. They wanted to see a display of worldly power, of self-preservation. They weren't disappointed in Jesus' lack of power, they just didn't like what He did with it.

God gave His Son to be trampled on. The Glory of Heaven was belittled by petty men who were worthy of no respect by any decent standards. This doesn't look to us like a wise use of power.

When Jesus was raised from the dead, He appeared to more than five hundred people, whom He sent out as witnesses. Five hundred is great, but why not five thousand? Why did Jesus draw a smaller crowd after His resurrection than before? Why didn't He appear to five million people? Why didn't He stick around a bit longer and travel the world?

Compared to what He could have done, sending five hundred witnesses seems pretty weak. But so did staying on the cross when He could have come down. God hides His power in weakness to protect it from the very kind of men who put Him on trial and had Him killed.

Here is another question: if leaving a handful of witnesses was such a bad strategy, why has their testimony been so powerfully accepted by so many for so long? From that first generation until now, people have met God through the preaching of Christ crucified. Multitudes have been happily willing to be put to death rather than to even pretend that the message wasn't true.

Paul said, in 2 Corinthians 13:4, *"For though He was crucified in weakness, yet He lives by the power of God. For we also are weak in Him, but we shall live with Him by the power of God toward you."*

The word of the cross continues to spread today by that same power. It has always worked and always will. The question is whether men and women will proclaim it as it is, or exchange it for something that seems more impressive.

Lesson #6: Until We See the Power of God's Weakness and the Weakness of Our Power, We Haven't Encountered the Wisdom of the Cross

Lesson #7:

The Message of the Cross Is Offensive, but If We Make It Plain, God Will Make It Beautiful

Because the foolishness of God is wiser than men, and the weakness of God is stronger than men.

1 Corinthians 1:25

Paul's language here expresses how different God is from us. There is no overlap between us and Him, as if our strongest point could be compared to His weakest.

When we encounter God in the message of the cross, we can't compare strength for strength and wisdom for wisdom. God's strength and wisdom don't even look like ours.

God is not just different from us by degrees, He's an utter stranger to us. This is what the cross tells us.

Mankind was created to reflect God's image and to be intimately acquainted with Him. But sin has so alienated us from God that He has become a stranger to us.

And we don't realize it. We are like Samson waking up after having had his hair cut. He tried to fight like he always did before, not realizing that his power was gone (see Judges 16). Likewise, we didn't think we were so alienated from God. We thought we might have disappointed Him, but we didn't think we were His enemies.

The cross shows us the damage sin has done to us. It reveals to us where we really stand in relation to God.

As we have seen (Lesson #4), Isaiah referred to the cross as a marvelous work and a wonder. In another place, however, he also called it a strange work. That's how it confronts us at first, not as wonderful but as strange.

Isaiah 28:21 says,

"For the Lord will rise up as at Mount Perazim,
He will be angry as in the Valley of Gibeon—
That He may do His work, His awesome work,
And bring to pass His act, His unusual act."

Here the work of God is referred to as *awesome* and *unusual.* Other translations of this verse use adjectives like *foreign, alien, peculiar,* and the word that is probably most often used in the English translations: *strange.*

Christians often sing, "This is the day that the Lord has made, I will rejoice and be glad in it." This line is taken from Psalm 118. When we sing "this is the day that the Lord has made," we are usually referring to whatever day is currently called "today." Every day is the day that the Lord has made, so we are not wrong when we sing this. Nevertheless, we can sing this line about "today" only because it is true of the day to which it originally refers.

Psalm 118:22-24 says, *"The stone which the builders rejected has become the chief cornerstone. This was the Lord's doing; it is marvelous in our eyes. This is the day the Lord has made; we will rejoice and be glad in it."*

This is a prophesy that the Christ would be glorified through suffering. The Israelites sang this psalm every year when they celebrated the Passover Feast. Jesus and His disciples probably sang this psalm together the night He was arrested. It was only Jesus, however, who knew what His disciples were really saying through the words of this psalm.

They were saying in prophesy what Paul would later say in Galatians 6:14: *"But God forbid that I should boast except in the cross of our Lord Jesus Christ, by whom the world has been crucified to me, and I to the world."*

By singing Psalm 118, the disciples were unwittingly boasting in the work of the cross and saying that it was marvelous in their eyes. God fulfilled this prophesy for them by making it marvelous in their eyes, so that they could truly boast in it.

At the time, however, it was anything but marvelous. When the stone became the chief cornerstone—when Jesus was raised from the dead—it was indeed glorious. But three days earlier, when that stone was rejected, the day seemed anything but marvelous, and no disciple of Jesus would have wanted to proclaim that God had made that day.

The writer of Hebrews said that *"it was fitting for Him, for whom are all things and by whom are all things, in bringing many sons to glory, to make the captain of their salvation perfect through sufferings."* (Hebrews 2:10)

Looking back more than thirty years later he could say, with the help of the Holy Spirit, *"it was fitting."* However, if he had been there when it happened, he would not have been able to say that. Christ's sufferings did not look fitting at all at the time. They looked like the most unfitting thing to ever happen.

The word of the cross is weakness and foolishness. It is offensive. It has always been resisted and always will be. Christ's crucifixion is ugly. You can't make it beautiful in people's eyes. You can't make it fitting or marvelous.

What you can do is to proclaim it as clearly as you can. Make it plain, and God will make it beautiful.

For two thousand years, the Holy Spirit has been fulfilling the words of Isaiah 29 and Psalm 118. He has been taking God's strange work and making it wonderful and marvelous in people's eyes. This is His job. He's good at it, He's faithful at it, and He's not going to stop now.

Lesson #7: The Message of the Cross Is Offensive, but If We Make It Plain, God Will Make It Beautiful

Lesson #8:

The Cross Isn't Biased, but We Are, and We Need to Be Aware of Our Biases

For you see your calling, brethren, that not many wise according to the flesh, not many mighty, not many noble, are called. But God has chosen the foolish things of the world to put to shame the wise, and God has chosen the weak things of the world to put to shame the things which are mighty; and the base things of the world and the things which are despised God has chosen, and the things which are not, to bring to nothing the things that are, that no flesh should glory in His presence.

1 Corinthians 1:26-29

Since the word of the cross is unusual, the church formed by the preaching of that word also looks unusual. Normally, when a group of people come together for the sake of a common interest, they have a lot of other things in common as well. But when God calls people by the word of the cross, He doesn't just call a certain kind. He calls all kinds, puts them together, and expects them to get along.

Paul said that there were *not many* who were mighty or noble in the church. He didn't say there were none.

There were some who were well-off or respected by society. Crispus was a synagogue ruler and Erastus was the treasurer of the city (Acts 18:8, Romans 16:23).

Most people in the Corinthian church were poor, although a few were rich. This is probably because most people in *Corinth* were poor, although a few were rich. As it was in Corinth, so it was in the church. Some were slaves, some were free. There were Romans, Greeks, and Jews. The Corinthian church represented a cross section of the city.

God doesn't discriminate against the poor, but He doesn't discriminate against the rich either. We know He wouldn't do that because it's against His own law. Leviticus 19:15 says, *"You shall do no injustice in judgment. You shall not be partial to the poor, nor honor the person of the mighty. In righteousness you shall judge your neighbor."*

The word of the cross is not about being contrary and unexpected for the sake of being contrary and unexpected, and it's not about favoring a certain class of people. The gospel doesn't discriminate. It meets people where they are and gathers them together. And the result never looks like what we would imagine.

Groucho Marx once said, "I don't want to belong to any club that would accept *me* as a member." This is a common approach to belonging to a church as well. Our standards for the ideal church are probably so high that we would disqualify ourselves from joining.

The reality of church life will put anybody's idealistic vision of church to the test. The Corinthians certainly tested Paul. When Paul first arrived in Corinth, the Lord spoke to him in a vision and told him to stay for a while, assuring him and saying, *"I have many people in this city"* (Acts 18:9-10). God told him this ahead of time. Perhaps, after a few months, Paul was tempted to ask Him, "Are You *sure* You got the right people?"

(This realistic view of the church always went hand in hand with another perspective on the church: not human idealism, but a heavenly point of view. We will consider this in Lesson #23.)

The gospel doesn't show partiality and it doesn't judge people by worldly standards. *We* do, however, and we need to train ourselves not to. This may require going out of our way to think about things differently than we normally do.

We tend to think of ourselves first, second, and third. Then we tend to think about other people using our own situation as a frame of reference. If we don't make enough money, we look at other people and wonder how much money they make. If we are lonely, we wonder if they are lonely. If we are looking for an apartment, we wonder how they found *their* apartment.

The word of the cross not only teaches us to think of others first, but also to look at ourselves more objectively, and not just through the lens of our present situation.

Consider, for example, Paul's counsel to the church in 1 Corinthians 7:20-23:

"Let each one remain in the same calling in which he was called. Were you called while a slave? Do not be concerned about it; but if you can be made free, rather use it. For he who is called in the Lord while a slave is the Lord's freedman. Likewise he who is called while free is Christ's slave. You were bought at a price; do not become slaves of men."

Paul reminds the slave that he is the Lord's free man—that he is spiritually free regardless of his natural circumstances. He then reminds the naturally free man that he is actually a slave of Christ.

Isn't the naturally free man also the Lord's free man spiritually? Of course he is, but he doesn't need to be reminded about that because he will automatically think of his spiritual situation in terms of his natural situation. That's his only frame of reference. He needs, therefore, to be reminded of his spiritual obligation to serve all men as Christ did.

Likewise, the one who is a slave to other men is also Christ's slave. But that is how he already sees himself in relation to Christ. He needs to be reminded of his spiritual freedom.

In both cases, Paul reminds believers to see themselves from a perspective that would not naturally occur to them. He is advising them to be aware of their own prejudices and to compensate for them if necessary.

The cross doesn't discriminate, but we do. We must have our minds transformed. When Paul exhorts them, in the verses above, *do not become slaves of men,* he means not to think like men normally think. It is in our thinking, our mindset, that we can become slaves of men even while we think we are free.

Consider your calling. Remember that God has chosen you, and don't view yourself through the labels, good or bad, that other people have put on you, or that you have put on yourself.

Lesson #8: The Cross Isn't Biased, but We Are, and We Need to Be Aware of Our Biases

Lesson #9:

We Always Receive More from God than We Realize at the Time

But of Him you are in Christ Jesus, who became for us wisdom from God—and righteousness and sanctification and redemption

1 Corinthians 1:30

Paul says that Christ Himself became our wisdom, but he doesn't stop there. He adds three more things that Christ became for us: righteousness, sanctification, and redemption. Paul could have added more things still. He could have continued for quite a long time. Christ became more for us than we have yet to understand.

What we mean by *salvation* and what God's means by it are not the same. God means what we mean, but also much more. The Bible gives us many words to help us understand our salvation, and each of those words means more to God than it does to us. Nevertheless, we want to understand them as best we can, and to always be growing in our understanding, however imperfect it may be.

Righteousness, sanctification, and *redemption* are precise words, and each one means something different yet related. It's good to study and ponder these words, but it's even better to hold fast to Christ, who is all of these things for you and more.

A man may simply know that he is guilty before God and needs forgiveness. He may never have heard of righteousness, sanctification, or redemption. Yet when he gets forgiveness, he gets all these things as well.

With God we always get more than we realize we are getting.

Righteousness, sanctification, and redemption are life-changing words. However, don't lose sight of those smaller yet also amazing words in this verse: *for us*.

Christ became *for us*. These words are just as power-ful. In fact, they give those other words their power by making them accessible to us.

Also, don't forget those other little words: *of Him*. That means God Himself. This is His doing.

And then there is that mind-boggling word *in*. You are not just near Christ, or even with Him. You are *in* Him.

The Bible should be studied in its entirety. Right-eousness, sanctification, and redemption are im-portant concepts to understand. But if someone were to somehow take these big words away from you, you would still have the gospel in the little words.

Of Him you are *in* Christ Jesus, who became *for us*!

Just think about that for the rest of your life. You'll never get to the bottom of it. Just try to establish exactly what these three words—*Christ for you*—mean to you. They'll always mean more to God than they do to you.

Not only is salvation more abundant and diverse than we can comprehend, it's also much simpler than we often make it out to be. In fact, I may be complicating matters by referring to righteousness, sanctification, and redemption as *things*. As Paul clearly tells us in the verse above, they're not *things,* they're *Christ*. We tend to de-personalize these concepts when thinking and talking about them. We need to be careful about this.

Watchman Nee once said, "Christianity is not any one thing which Christ gives to me; Christianity is Christ giving himself to me."[1] Nee made this statement in a sermon entitled, "Christ is God's Everything," which is contained in a book called, *Christ the Sum of All Spiritual Things*.

He went on to say, "As long as our sanctification, redemption, regeneration, power, grace and gift remain as objects, we are still standing on the borderline of Christianity. But when we see these not as things but the Lord himself, we begin to know God

---

[1] Nee, Watchman. *Christ the Sum of All Spiritual Things* (Christian Fellowship Publishers)

and enter into God's eternal purpose. Hereafter it is always He, never things."[2]

God has met our needs by giving us His Son. He wants us to trust Him to provide for us everything we need in this life, spiritual and material. This trust will grow in us as we come to understand that what we really need is "always He, never things."

Lesson #9: We Always Receive More from God than We Realize at the Time

---

[2] Nee, Watchman. *Christ the Sum of All Spiritual Things* (Christian Fellowship Publishers)

Lesson #10:

The Message of the Cross Is an Entryway into Deep Knowledge of God

— that, as it is written, "He who glories, let him glory in the Lord."

1 Corinthians 1:31

Until now, Paul's focus has been on the word of the cross as God's strange work, the shocking and offensive message from God that reveals our alienation from Him and our enmity against Him. The God of the cross is mysterious and unknowable.

Furthermore, the cross is ugly. The message is unattractive and offensive. To the eyes of the world it looks weak and foolish. It's like a door through which no one would ever want to enter.

But Paul's discourse is not finished yet. There is more to the story. The message of the cross may be like a door that looks uninviting, but once a person enters that door, it truly leads to the holy places of God. God takes His strange work and makes it marvelous in our eyes. He opens our eyes to see the truth, to begin to see things as He sees them.

So far, Paul has been describing the message of the cross as it appears from the outside, looking in. *Try-*

ing to look in, I should say, for you can't see into the cross. You can't see through it or around it. You can only be confronted by it, and by the lengths to which God has gone to reach you.

Paul had come to Corinth and preached this word of the cross unflinchingly, and many believed. They had been on the outside, looking in. Paul had brought them in. He is now writing to remind them what is theirs and what they are missing when they fall back into pettiness and worldly thinking.

Paul will go on, in the next several verses, to describe the depths of the knowledge of God which has been given to us in Christ Jesus. He has begun here with a quotation from the prophet Jeremiah. He quotes just a few words, but no doubt he has the whole passage in mind, for it echoes what he has been saying about worldly wisdom and power.

Here is Jeremiah 9:23-24, the passage that Paul is quoting from:

"Thus says the Lord:

'Let not the wise man glory in his wisdom,
Let not the mighty man glory in his might,
Nor let the rich man glory in his riches;
But let him who glories glory in this,
That he understands and knows Me,
That I am the Lord, exercising lovingkindness, judgment, and
righteousness in the earth.
For in these I delight,' says the Lord."

Jeremiah says that we should glory not just because the Lord exists, but because we understand and know Him. So, despite the strangeness of the God who reveals Himself to us by the work of the cross, it is still possible to understand and know Him.

There are at least three levels of understanding God that we can learn from this passage of Jeremiah.

The first level is to know what God does. He exercises lovingkindness, judgment, and righteousness in the earth. In order to begin to know God in this way, we must learn what these words mean. But, as we have seen in the previous lesson, we should be careful not to see these things as abstract concepts separated from Jesus Christ Himself.

If the first level of understanding is to know what God does, the second level is to know why He does it. As I said earlier (Lesson #5), the gospel doesn't reveal what impresses God, but what pleases Him. To understand that God delights in certain things—which is not merely a delight in *things*, but actually in *Christ*—is to know that He has a personality. He is not just an impersonal force in the universe.

The third level of understanding God is to delight in the same things—in the same Person—that He delights in. This understanding-by-delighting comes only through the gospel of Jesus Christ.

In the cross, God has exercised *"lovingkindness, judgment, and righteousness in the earth."* If you can glory in the cross of Christ, you are delighting in these things with God, although you may have only a rudimentary understanding of what these words mean.

Like Jeremiah, the prophet Isaiah also encouraged the people to seek to understand God. Isaiah 1:18 teaches us the first step in getting to know God:

"'Come now, and let us reason together,'
Says the Lord,
'Though your sins are like scarlet,
They shall be as white as snow;
Though they are red like crimson,
They shall be as wool.'"

Here is an invitation to reason together with God. The promise given in this invitation is that our sins will be washed away. This promise is not held out as the final agreement that will be reached after we have reasoned with God. This is the starting point. This is God's initial offer: your sins are great, but He will forgive them. Come to Him on these terms or else reasoning with Him will never even begin.

Reasoning with God doesn't mean that you think like you think, God think like He thinks, and you come to a compromise. Reasoning with God means giving up the way you think and being taught by God how to think. Reasoning with God doesn't lead to compromise, but to agreement—and then to fellowship, and ultimately, to friendship.

Lesson #10: The Message of the Cross Is an Entryway into Deep Knowledge of God

Lesson #11:

If We Judge the Messenger by Worldly Standards, We Will Miss the Glory of the Message

And I, brethren, when I came to you, did not come with excellence of speech or of wisdom declaring to you the testimony of God. For I determined not to know anything among you except Jesus Christ and Him crucified. I was with you in weakness, in fear, and in much trembling. And my speech and my preaching were not with persuasive words of human wisdom, but in demonstration of the Spirit and of power, that your faith should not be in the wisdom of men but in the power of God.

1 Corinthians 2:1-5

As we have seen, Paul is transitioning from talking about the word of the cross from an outside perspective to talking about it from an inside perspective. Here he is reminding the Corinthians that he had come to them and brought them in from the outside.

We have compared the word of the cross to an unattractive door. Another metaphor we could use is the temple of God. When the Corinthians first believed the gospel, they came from the Outer Court, where they were bystanders, into the Holy Place, where they have fellowship with God.

Outside of the cross, people see the message as foolish and weak. On the inside, they find riches and glory. This spiritual wealth, made available by the gospel, was also part of Paul's message. It was what made all his suffering worthwhile. He got to offer people unimaginable eternal glory.

In Ephesians 1:13, Paul called his message *"the gospel of your salvation."* In another place he called it *"the gospel of the glory of Christ"* (2 Corinthians 4:4). Just as your salvation is good news, the glory of Christ is also good news. Your salvation and His glory are part of the same gospel.

In Ephesians 3:8, Paul marveled at the privilege of preaching this gospel: *"To me, who am less than the least of all the saints, this grace was given, that I should preach among the Gentiles the unsearchable riches of Christ..."*

The word *preach,* in this verse, means to evangelize, which means to announce good news. The fact that Christ's greatness is unsearchable is good news for us. It means we have a lot to look forward to. We will never be bored in heaven and we never need to be bored on earth.

Paul continued in the next verse (Ephesians 3:9): *"and to make all see what is the fellowship of the mystery, which from the beginning of the ages has been hidden in God who created all things through Jesus Christ..."*

So, it was a mystery about unsearchable riches, a mystery that had always been hidden (not just hidden, but hidden *in God*). Yet, despite the unsearchable depths of this mystery, Paul was confident that he could *make all see* it, or, as other translations put it, bring it to light and make it plain to see.

No wonder Paul didn't rely upon eloquent speech and impressive vocabulary to preach his gospel. There are no words eloquent enough to do the job that he was given to do. The *"demonstration of the Spirit and of power"* was necessary, not just to prove to prove the truth of the message, but to reveal the glory of it.

When Christ came into this world, He came as an average-looking man. There was nothing about His physical appearance, in and of itself, that set Him apart from other men. Therefore, those who did not worship Him as God considered Him as just another man.

Christ still comes to people every day in the proclamation of the gospel. But the gospel comes by means of human messengers speaking human words. When it is not believed, it is looked at as just another religion among many.

When Paul came to Corinth, he looked like just another traveling teacher among many such men competing for the Corinthians' attention and respect. The difference with Paul is that he was untrained in the kind of rhetoric that the Corinthians looked for in a speaker. When God sent the gospel to Corinth by means of Paul, He sent it in a very unimpressive package.

Yet there is not messenger on earth who could be impressive enough, in terms of natural charisma, to impress upon people the true greatness of the gospel. The message will always be infinitely more glorious than the messenger.

When we give up on the wisdom and power of this world, and allow the cross of Christ to come between us and the world, then true knowledge of God and spiritual power become available to us. God leads us into a greater realization of this power through diverse people and circumstances. All these people and circumstances serve as teachers to us by the providence of God.

Sometimes we must recognize the teacher before we can learn the lesson. Sometimes recognizing the teacher is the hardest part of the lesson.

Like He did for the Corinthians, God often sends us gifts hidden in packages that we do not find naturally appealing. The good news is that He wants us to receive His gifts and He will teach us not to overlook them.

Lesson #11: If We Judge the Messenger by Worldly Standards, We Will Miss the Glory of the Message

Lesson #12:

The Wisdom of God, Although Violently Opposed, Brings Peace

However, we speak wisdom among those who are mature, yet not the wisdom of this age, nor of the rulers of this age, who are coming to nothing. But we speak the wisdom of God in a mystery, the hidden wisdom which God ordained before the ages for our glory, which none of the rulers of this age knew; for had they known, they would not have crucified the Lord of glory.

1 Corinthians 2:6-8

We might have expected that the rulers of this age would have ignored the Lord of glory, because they didn't have the wisdom to recognize Him. But, far from ignoring Him, they persecuted and killed Him.

The wisdom of this age is not neutral, and it is not passive. It manifested itself in violence in the crucifixion of Jesus, and it has violently opposed the gospel ever since. The wisdom of this age will always lead to violence eventually, no matter how peaceful it sounds.

The hidden wisdom of God, on the other hand, comes from peace and leads to peace. It is peaceful, but it is not passive. It is active. It is not silent; it makes itself seen and heard. And it is usually seen before it is heard.

James 3:13 says, *"Who is wise and understanding among you? Let him show by good conduct that his works are done in the meekness of wisdom."* Beware of anything that sounds like deep spiritual wisdom, but can only be heard in a person's words and not seen in their conduct. According to James, wisdom is like faith: it is seen in a person's behavior.

James was writing to his fellow Jewish believers at a time when there was open hostility against them from unbelieving Jews, sometimes persecution. According to historical reports, James himself was killed for his faith in Christ.

Yet James counseled these followers of Jesus to walk in the meekness of wisdom. He also warned them that *"the wrath of man does not produce the righteousness of God"* (James 1:20).

These people had much that they could have been angry about because of the way they had been treated. If they had been angry because they were being persecuted, their anger may have seemed justified.

But here James is warning them that anger is not justified by its object, but by its source. There is so much evil and injustice in the world that it is easy to get angry, especially when people do terrible things and seem to get away with it. Christians can be so moved by this anger that they repay evil for evil and justify it because they are angry at the right things.

But being angry at the right things does not make our anger righteous.

James is not talking about the object of the anger, but the source. The anger (or wrath) that *originates* from people will never bring about the righteousness that *originates* from God.

Paul, likewise, warned the church in Rome to stay out of God's way and not try to do His job: *"Bless those who persecute you; bless and do not curse...Repay no one evil for evil...do not avenge yourselves, but rather give place to wrath; for it is written, "Vengeance is Mine, I will repay."* (Romans 13:17-19)

President Theodore Roosevelt summarized United States foreign policy this way: "Speak softly and carry a big stick." How much more freedom do we have to speak softly when we know that it is God Himself who is carrying the stick?

At the same time, speaking softly does not mean compromise. It is right to speak out against evil and injustice. Consider Stephen in the book of Acts, the first martyr of the church. We are told that he was *"full of the Holy Spirit and wisdom,"* and that the opponents of the gospel *"were not able to resist the wisdom and the Spirit by which he spoke."* (Acts 6:3,10)

Yet Stephen didn't just speak softly. Wisdom led him to issue a severe rebuke against the religious leaders of Jerusalem when he was on trial: *"You stiff-necked and uncircumcised in heart and ears! You always resist the Holy Spirit; as your fathers did, so do you. Which of the prophets did your fathers not persecute? And they killed those who foretold the coming of the Just One, of whom you now have become the betrayers and murderers, who have received the law by the direction of angels and have not kept it."* (Acts 7:51-53)

These are not gentle words by any means. But consider the context. Before Stephen spoke these words, he had earned a reputation in the church because of his godly character. For this reason, he was given more responsibility in the church, to serve the people. He served faithfully, and became even more well-known for the miracles that God worked through him.

Now consider what happened right after Stephen spoke these words. He was stoned to death while praying for the same people he had just rebuked: *"And they stoned Stephen as he was calling on God and saying, 'Lord Jesus, receive my spirit.' Then he knelt down and cried out with a loud voice, 'Lord, do not charge them with this sin.' And when he had said this, he fell asleep."* (Acts 7:59-60)

Stephen's words of rebuke were bold and strong, but they weren't cheap. They were backed up by his actions, both before and after he spoke them. So, by all means, speak out against evil and injustice, but if you want to achieve the maximum effect, earn the authority to be heard and be ready to die interceding for the same people you speak out against.

Lesson #12: The Wisdom of God, Although Violently Opposed, Brings Peace

Lesson #13:

The Spirit of God Reveals What the Heart Cannot Imagine

But as it is written:

**"Eye has not seen, nor ear heard,
Nor have entered into the heart of man
The things which God has prepared for those
who love Him."**

**But God has revealed them to us through His
Spirit.**

1 Corinthians 2:9-10a

There is something missing from the human heart.
There are things that have not yet entered into the
heart, but that the heart nevertheless longs for.

Romans 8:26 reveals a weakness that all Christians
experience: *"Likewise the Spirit helps us in our weaknesses.
For we don't know what we should pray for as we ought, but
the Spirit Himself makes intercession for us with groanings
which cannot be uttered."*

Not knowing what to pray for is a weakness. We
often don't know how to pray. This may be due to an
especially difficult trial, or a complicated situation we
have never faced before. Any circumstance of life

can reveal this weakness in us, but such situations don't reveal the depths of the weakness or its true nature.

The weakness Paul is talking about in Romans 8:26 is more than a lack of wisdom concerning how to pray about a particular situation. That is a manifestation of the weakness, but the weakness itself is deeper.

Consider the passage leading up to Romans 8:26. Verse 18, for example, says that *"the sufferings of this present time are not worthy to be compared with the glory which shall be revealed in us."*

So, this is a teaching about the glory of the age to come. It is about a glory that will be revealed in the saints, a glory that all of creation is waiting for. And not only that, *"but we also who have the firstfruits of the Spirit, even we ourselves groan within ourselves, eagerly waiting for the adoption, the redemption of our body. For we were saved in this hope, but hope that is seen is not hope; for why does one still hope for what he sees? But if we hope for what we do not see, we eagerly wait for it with perseverance."* (Romans 8:23-25)

Then, after saying that, Paul says that we are weak because we don't know what to pray for. What we are supposed to pray for is what we are eagerly waiting for: the glory of the age to come. But how can we pray for it if we can't even imagine it?

We lack the knowledge of the glory of the age to come. We not only lack the knowledge, we lack the capacity to know such knowledge. This is where the Holy Spirit helps us.

The Spirit gives us a knowledge of something that our eyes can't see and our hearts can't imagine. How appropriate it is then, that this help comes with groanings that can't be uttered.

The Holy Spirit helps us by making intercession for us. The Holy Spirit can intercede perfectly because He possesses perfect knowledge of the glory. The glory of God makes our intercession increasingly effective.

We can see this in the life of Moses.

Moses was a great intercessor. He drew near to God and interceded for the nation of Israel, saving it from destruction.

Exodus 32-33 tells the story of the golden calf. When Moses came down from Mount Sinai after receiving the law, he discovered that the Israelites had already turned to idolatry. It was a disaster. It looked like everything that God had done in delivering Israel out of Egypt would be for nothing. God told Moses that His presence would not go with the Israelites any further.

Moses turned things around by his influence with God and his self-sacrificing leadership. He asked God that His presence would continue to go with them. Exodus 33:17 says, *"So the Lord said to Moses, 'I will also do this thing that you have spoken; for you have found grace in My sight, and I know you by name.'"*

Moses won that day. He had a great victory in prayer. At the same time, however, his work was only beginning. He must have realized more than ever just how hard his job was going to be—too hard for any human being to do. It called for a wisdom that he didn't have, as well as patience, stamina, courage, faith, hope, and love.

He could have asked for any one of these things. He needed all of them and more. He didn't even know what he would need in the days to come.

He didn't ask for any one of these things, however. Instead, he asked for all of them. In one sentence, with a handful of words, he asked for everything he would need to finish his job, even though he couldn't imagine what he would need.

"Please," he said to God, *"show me Your glory."* (Exodus 33:18)

What God reveals to us by His Spirit is the glory that He has ordained for us before the world began, a glory that will be revealed in us in the age to come. In the revelation of this glory, God gives us the wisdom we need to do what He has called us to do. Indeed, He will supply all our needs according to His riches in glory (see Philippians 4:19).

Lesson #13: The Spirit of God Reveals What the Heart Cannot Imagine

Lesson #14:

The Message of the Cross Guards Holiness and Leads to Intimate Fellowship with God

For the Spirit searches all things, yes, the deep things of God. For what man knows the things of a man except the spirit of the man which is in him? Even so no one knows the things of God except the Spirit of God.

1 Corinthians 2:10b-11

The Corinthians had been evaluating ministers of the gospel by their appearance and their appeal to the carnal mind. They were looking at the surface of things. Paul explained to them that this was worldly wisdom, also called the wisdom of man or the wisdom of the flesh.

This was a relapse in their thinking. It was not how they had come to know God in the first place. In fact, they could never have come to know God by thinking about Him this way.

Paul has reminded them that he first came to them proclaiming Jesus Christ and Him crucified. This proclamation challenged the worldly wisdom of the Corinthians, just as it does to all of us. In the word of the cross, we are confronted by a strange and unknowable God. We are forced to confess that we have not known Him at all, but have been alienated from Him and at odds with Him.

This is what had happened to the Corinthians when Paul preached the cross to them. But now Paul is describing, not the wisdom of man, but the wisdom of God. Paul had brought the Corinthians into the temple of God, metaphorically speaking. They had been on the outside, strangers to the ways of God. Paul had brought them to the knowledge of God by the word of the cross.

Paul began his discussion by describing how things appear from outside the temple, as it were. Then he came into the Holy Place, where the Spirit reveals God's glory. Now, in this passage, he is moving into the inner chamber of the temple, what was called the Holy of Holies.

On the outside, we learned that God cannot be known as other men can be known. Now, on the inside, we learn that we can know Him more intimately than we could ever know another person.

"For what man knows the things of a man except the spirit of the man which is in him?" (1 Corinthians 2:11)

There is a limit to how well we can get to know one another in this world. A man can try all day long to explain himself to you, but it would be so much more effective it he could simply take his spirit and put it into you for a few minutes.

You would instantly know more about that man than could ever be put into words. His life experiences, his personality, his nature—none of that would have to be explained to you. It could be comprehended in a moment if he could just take his spirit and put in into you.

Of course, such an experience is impossible (thank God!).

However, it is not impossible when it comes to God. Although God is different from us, God is Spirit. Although we can't know Him in the same way we know other people, we can actually know Him better. The divine-human relationship can be closer than any human-human relationship.

It *can be* closer. That doesn't mean it always is. As I said, we are now in the Holy of Holies, and we are speaking of things that are difficult to put into words and easy to misunderstand.

This topic is subject to a lot of abuse. As we will soon see, Paul didn't talk much about these things to the Corinthians when he first met them because they were carnal. They were immature believers, and an immature person can deceive himself into thinking that he knows God a lot better than he really does. That's why the word of the cross is always necessary, even in the Holy of Holies.

The word of the cross is not just a message that leads to one's initial salvation, after which it can then be discarded as one progresses into a deeper knowledge of God. Far from it! The word of the cross is your only hope of escaping self-deception as long as you live in this world. The word of the cross must always be with you, reminding you that any intimacy you will ever experience with God is His gift, and that He sought you before you ever sought Him.

One of the true marks of intimacy with God is reverence for His holiness, as opposed to casual presumption. The cross preserves this reverence from corruption. So, although the message of the cross is itself subject to ridicule and contempt, it actually guards God's holiness.

If you truly know God you will boast in the cross of Christ. You will glory in it every day as your only hope and salvation.

You will also be more concerned with how much you love God than with how well you know Him. You will never know Him more than you love Him. So if you make sure that you are loving Him with all that you've got, you can be sure that you are also coming to know Him as well, and that He will make Himself known to you, and you won't deceive yourself into thinking that you know Him when you don't.

The question to ask yourself, therefore, is not, "How well do I know Him?" but, "How much do I love Him?" This is, after all, what Jesus called the greatest commandment (see Matthew 22:37-38).

The next question you could ask yourself is if your love for God is affecting the way you treat people, and whether or not you are loving your neighbor as yourself, which is, of course, the second greatest commandment (Matthew 22:39).

Lesson #14: The Message of the Cross Guards Holiness and Leads to Intimate Fellowship with God

Lesson #15:

The Spirit of God Reveals to Us Our True Calling, Which Is Always a Call to Greatness

Now we have received, not the spirit of the world, but the Spirit who is from God, that we might know the things that have been freely given to us by God.

1 Corinthians 2:12

As we saw earlier in our study, we always receive more from God than we realize at the time (Lesson #9). God gives us gifts that we can recognize and receive, but each gift also comes with further blessings that we do not discern at first. The Holy Spirit, therefore, helps us to realize what we have been given. He also saves us from the tragedy of unfulfilled potential.

Jesus always has enough. When He had just five loaves of bread, He fed more than five thousand people. Not only did He feed them, but there was bread left over. In John 6:12, we are told that after the crowd had eaten, Jesus instructed His disciples, saying, *"Gather up the fragments that remain, so that nothing is lost."*

Jesus wasn't afraid of running out of bread. He wanted to collect the leftovers simply because He hates waste. Now, if that is how He feels about bread, how must He feel about the gifts and potential that He has placed within each of His followers?

Paul told his friend Philemon that he was praying for him with the following goal in mind: *"that the sharing of your faith may become effective by the acknowledgment of every good thing which is in you in Christ Jesus."* (Philemon 1:6)

Great things have been freely given to us by God, even at the moment when we first believed. Even before that, actually, for Paul had said, in 1 Corinthians 1:7, that he was talking about a hidden wisdom which God has ordained *before the ages* for our glory.

People love a story about a seemingly average person who discovers that they are actually someone of great importance. Whether it's a farm-boy on a distant planet who is the secret son of a fallen Jedi knight, a medieval peasant who pulls a sword out of a rock, accidentally proving himself to be king, or just a spy with amnesia, the formula is used repeatedly because it works so well.

This is a marvelous thing about Christianity: everybody who trusts in Jesus turns out to be secretly important, someone chosen ahead of time, someone with a great destiny to fulfill.

The gospel is about Jesus. We have seen that it is called the *"gospel of the glory of Christ"* (2 Corinthians 4:4). But the gospel also tells us that Jesus came to *"purify for Himself His own special people"* (Titus 2:14). Each one of these special people represents an amazing story about hidden greatness and a secret identity.

To believe the gospel is to hear a personal call to greatness that was spoken over your life before you were born. This is quite different from the greatness of the world, as measured by the wisdom of the world. It's a different kind of greatness but it's also a vastly greater kind. To use the kind of language that Paul has been using in 1 Corinthians, we could say that the ordinariness of God is greater than the greatness of man. There is nothing ordinary about it, in other words. There are no ordinary, run-of-the-mill saints. God doesn't make them.

The tragedy is that sometimes even Christians them-selves remain unaware of this call to greatness. Many of the Corinthians believers remained ignorant of this call to spiritual greatness, no doubt, for they were still captivated by human greatness.

There are also many saints in every generation who heed this call, follow it with all their hearts, and labor for the rest of their lives, unrecognized and unappre-ciated. Spiritual greatness often goes unnoticed in this world. Nevertheless, such people are noticed by heaven and are kept "hidden in the bosom of the Church," in the words of French Jesuit priest Jean-Pierre De Caussade.

De Caussade pointed this out in some letters written to a group of nuns in the 1730's, letters meant only for those obscure laborers, but later collected and published as a book, *Abandonment to Divine Providence*. In those letters, De Caussade assured them that, although they were not famous in this world, heaven would not allow their work to go unrecognized.

"Many saints," he said, "are raised up by God for the salvation of souls and to enlighten the most backward. Such saints were the prophets and the apostles and all those others who have been and will be chosen by God to illuminate the world. There will always be such saints, as there have always been. But there is also a multitude of others hidden in the bosom of the Church who are destined to shine only in heaven, and so in this life they live and die in complete obscurity."[3]

If you let the Spirit teach you about the greatness of your salvation, and if you dedicate yourself to living a life worthy of that greatness, then your life will be heroic. You may not get the credit until the credits roll, but you can be sure that your labor will not go unnoticed where it counts.

Lesson #15: The Spirit of God Reveals to Us Our True Calling, Which Is Always a Call to Greatness

---

[3] De Caussade, Jean-Pierre, *Abandonment to Divine Providence (Image Classics)* (The Crown Publishing Group), (p. 65)

Lesson #16:

The Truth Is Meant to Be Spiritually Tasted, Not Just Mentally Understood

These things we also speak, not in words which man's wisdom teaches but which the Holy Spirit teaches, comparing spiritual things with spiritual. But the natural man does not receive the things of the Spirit of God, for they are foolishness to him; nor can he know them, because they are spiritually discerned.

1 Corinthians 2:13-14

The phrase, *"comparing spiritual things with spiritual,"* represents three words in Greek which are rendered in various ways by the different English translations. The Amplified Bible sort of covers all the bases: *"combining and interpreting spiritual truths with spiritual language [to those who possess the Holy Spirit]."*

Regardless of how we translate this phrase, we want to make sure we don't misunderstand the word *spiritual*. Some people, even Christians, think *spiritual* signifies a realm of existence somewhere near *emotional* and just a few steps shy of *make-believe*. This is a poor understanding. It is the result of a worldly mindset.

People tend to think of that which is untouched and unseen as unreal. A. W. Tozer pointed out this problem in 1948, in his book *The Pursuit of God:*

"At the root of the Christian life lies belief in the invisible. The object of the Christian's faith is unseen reality.

"Our uncorrected thinking, influenced by the blindness of our natural hearts and the intrusive ubiquity of visible things, tends to draw a contrast between the spiritual and the real; but actually no such contrast exists. The antithesis lies elsewhere: between the real and the imaginary, between the spiritual and the material, between the temporal and the eternal; but between the spiritual and the real, never. The spiritual is real."[4]

This is a helpful reminder not to draw a contrast where none exists. If we think material things are more real than spiritual things, we will lose our focus and risk greater deception.

This is not the only misplaced antithesis we need to look out for, however. I would like to point out another one. It's the contrast between doctrine and spiritual things. According to this dichotomy, *doctrine* refers to theological information derived from the Bible, and *spiritual* refers to practical teaching about how to be a more Christ-like person or about how to

---

[4] Tozer, A. W. (Aiden Wilson), *The Pursuit of God* (Christian Publications, Inc., Harrisburg, PA, 1948), chapter four

pray or how to understand experiences such as dreams, visions, prophecies, etc.

If the aim of this dichotomy is to insist that experiences be judged in the light of what the Bible clearly teaches, this is a good goal. As we will see later in our study, Paul warned the Corinthians *"not to think beyond what is written"* (1 Corinthians 4:6).

The problem with this distinction between doctrine and spiritual things is that it doesn't do justice to biblical doctrine. It implies that doctrine, while necessary for the soul and good for the mind, is something other than spiritual. In reality, all doctrine is spiritual, and all doctrine is meant to experienced, not just understood.

God is good. That's a biblical doctrine. Any book about the attributes of God should convince you, in your mind, that goodness is one of those attributes. But I don't think that's what Peter had in mind when he asked, in 1 Peter 2:3, if the church had tasted that the Lord is good (or gracious, kind, or bountiful, as various translations put it). The goodness of God is a doctrine *and* a spiritual experience.

Eschatology should be studied and understood. But the writer of Hebrews meant more than that when he reminded the believers that they had tasted the powers of the age to come (Hebrews 6:5). Eschatology is a theological category *and* a spiritual experience.

The same is true for all biblical doctrine. If God had given us only the knowledge of the truth, it would not have been enough for us. He has also given us the love of the truth (2 Thessalonians 2:10). When we love the truth that we know, we enter into it in a deeper way.

Although the natural man does not receive these things, the Corinthians *had* received them, believed them, and rejoiced in them. But they were still immature, and they still conformed their thinking to the wisdom of the world. As we will soon see in our study, Paul could not talk to them as to mature believers. The things he has been discussing in these verses, about the hidden wisdom of God, were things they were not ready to hear.

They would not have rejected these ideas, like unbelievers would have. Rather, they would have misunderstood and abused them, making them a cause for further division. They would have argued with each other about what teachings are more spiritual than others and what the deep things of God really are. (Does God have any shallow things?)

They would have talked a lot about these things, and boasted in them, without first getting a good spiritual taste of them. They already had the tendency to do this with the truth, and Paul had to warn them, later in the letter, that their knowledge lacked love. Love builds up, in part because it also lays a deep foundation. Knowledge without love, on the other hand, simply puffs up (see 1 Corinthians 8:1).

Biblical doctrine is not given to us simply to be known, but also to be loved and to stir up love within us—and not just love as an emotion, but also love as a spiritual experience.

Lesson #16: The Truth Is Meant to Be Spiritually Tasted, Not Just Mentally Understood

Lesson #17:

The Wisdom of God Helps Us to Understand the World, and at the Same Time, Makes Us Hard to Understand

But he who is spiritual judges all things, yet he himself is rightly judged by no one. For "who has known the mind of the Lord that he may instruct Him?" But we have the mind of Christ.

1 Corinthians 2:15-16

Here Paul is quoting Isaiah 40:13. He also quotes that passage in Romans. Let's look first at the way he uses it there, in Romans 11:33-36:

"Oh, the depth of the riches both of the wisdom and knowledge of God! How unsearchable are His judgments and His ways past finding out!

'For who has known the mind of the Lord?
Or who has become His counselor?'
'Or who has first given to Him
And it shall be repaid to him?'

For of Him and through Him and to Him are all things, to whom be glory forever. Amen."

Paul's point here is that, in this life, there are things about God we cannot understand with our minds.

We dare not presume to have explored all the way to the bottom of God's mind and figured Him out.

That was in Romans. Here in 1 Corinthians, Paul says something different. He quotes that same passage from Isaiah and then adds, *"But we have the mind of Christ."*

That's a big "but." Paul is not taking back what he said in Romans, but he is adding something important here. (I don't mean that literally. 1 Corinthians was actually written before Romans.)

In 1 Corinthians, Paul is looking at things from a different angle because he is talking about a different subject. He is not contradicting what he says in Romans 11:33-36. The mind of God still cannot be looked into. God has not given us that ability. But the Spirit who searches the depths of God has given to us the ability to look out from God's mind, in the sense that we are reconciled to God and taught to see things from His perspective.

Remember that no matter how closely we think we have come to know God, the word of the cross stays with us to remind us not to presume to have figured Him out (see Lesson #14). It keeps us in our proper place before God, in humility and reverence. That same word of the cross, when we submit to it, also gives us the mind of Christ. As a result, although we don't see *into* God's mind, we see *out from* it.

Jesus Christ lived on this earth in perfect agreement with His Father. The Holy Spirit teaches us to see the world the way Jesus saw it. This is not the same thing as searching God's mind and figuring Him out, but it is still quite mind-boggling when you think about it.

Imagine an ice cream shop on a hot day. There may be several people there who see the place differently because they are looking at it from different perspectives. For example, a mother is there with her child. She is looking at the prices, the child is looking at the flavors. The employees are looking at the clock. A health inspector and a thief walk in. They are each going to notice different things about that ice cream shop.

Now imagine the founder and owner of the ice cream shop walks in. He would view things according to his original vision for that shop. He alone would know if things were as they should be, according to his purpose in opening the shop.

Likewise, Jesus views the world with its original purpose in mind. He does not look at the world the way we do, and it is we who need to change our perspective. The Holy Spirit gives us the gift of seeing the world the way Jesus does.

For this reason, worldly people look at believers and can't figure them out. This is behind Paul's statement that a spiritual person *"is rightly judged by no one."*

Yet that same spiritual person *"judges all things."* That doesn't seem fair.

The New Testament describes different kinds of judging. Some judging we should do and some we shouldn't; some we can and some we can't. In the letter of 1 Corinthians alone, Paul talks about several different kinds of judging. So, what does he mean in this passage?

Because the mind of Christ has been given to us, we can rightly understand the world around us. The gospel gives us the objective truth by which we can make sense of the world. We can't judge other men's motives, but we can know that all men are sinners. Unless the Holy Spirit gives us a special revelation, we can't know other peoples' secrets, but can we can know that God knows and that He cares. We can't fathom God's judgments, but we can be sure that He is merciful and righteous.

We can put the world around us in its proper context and view it from the right perspective. It is in this sense that we can "judge all things."

C. S. Lewis made a similar point in one of his well-known quotations. (It is from a message titled, "Is Theology Poetry?" which can be found in the book, *The Weight of Glory*.) He said, "I believe in Christianity as I believe that the sun has risen, not only because I see it, but because by it I see everything else."[5]

The truth of the gospel lights up the world for us, so we can see things more clearly.

---

[5] Lewis, C. S. *The Weight of Glory (Collected Letters of C.S. Lewis)* (HarperCollins)

Yet we ourselves are not clearly seen in this world. Because we have the mind of Christ directing and motivating us according to the wisdom of the cross, and because that wisdom is foolishness to worldly-minded people, therefore they can't make sense of the way we live our lives. They cannot "rightly judge us."

Jesus said, in John 3:8, *"The wind blows where it wishes, and you hear the sound of it, but cannot tell where it comes from and where it goes. So is everyone who is born of the Spirit."*

Everyone who is born of the Spirit and led by the Spirit demonstrates the wisdom of the Spirit. Those who judge according to the flesh couldn't judge the wisdom of the Spirit even if they wanted to, because they can't understand it. Neither, therefore, can they understand you.

Lesson #17: The Wisdom of God Helps Us to Understand the World, and at the Same Time, Makes Us Hard to Understand

Lesson #18:

The Word of God Speaks to Us at Our Level of Maturity and, at the Same Time, Challenges Us to Grow

And I, brethren, could not speak to you as to spiritual people but as to carnal, as to babes in Christ. I fed you with milk and not with solid food; for until now you were not able to receive it, and even now you are still not able; for you are still carnal. For where there are envy, strife, and divisions among you, are you not carnal and behaving like mere men? For when one says, "I am of Paul," and another, "I am of Apollos," are you not carnal?

1 Corinthians 3:1-4

If the previous section of 1 Corinthians was a trip into the Holy of Holies, these verses mark a rude return to the Outer Court.

The contrast between this passage and the one that precedes it matches the contrast between the wealth of spiritual gifts that had been given to the Corinthians and their continuing immaturity. The divisiveness and competition among them revealed that they were still looking on the surface appearance of things and not seeing the world with the mind of Christ.

In his brief discussion of the hidden wisdom of God (1 Corinthians 2:6-16), Paul had given them a glimpse of what they were missing out on. They could have been communing with God, but instead they were arguing with each other.

Paul could have expanded on these ideas, further describing the hidden wisdom of God and how the Holy Spirit searches the divine depths and communicates to our spirits glorious things that words cannot express. Such talk, however, would have been wasted on the Corinthians. It is not what they needed to hear at the time.

It could have been different, though. Paul had lived in Corinth for 18 months. By this time, they should have been advanced in their understanding of these things. Instead, they were taking one another to court, getting drunk at the Lord's Supper, debating whether or not there will be a resurrection of the dead, and opening tolerating a man sleeping with his father's wife.

It didn't have to be that way, however. And if the Corinthians had been more mature, the letter that Paul wrote to them would have looked different.

1 Corinthians was, in part, a response to some questions that the Corinthians had sent to Paul. We know this because Paul says, at one point, *"Now concerning the things of which you wrote to me..."* (1 Corinthians 7:1).

Imagine that the Corinthians had been much more mature, and that Paul had been speaking to them as mature believers all along. Their questions would have been different, and Paul's letter back to them would also have been different.

Imagine if they had written to Paul saying, "Paul, we have been studying those passages of Isaiah that you have quoted in your teaching, but what about these other passages? Explain to us the parts of Isaiah that you did not quote? We have been meditating on the things you have told us about the glory of Christ and the hidden wisdom of God. Please tell us more about these things."

Imagine what 1 Corinthians would look like if they had asked questions like these.

2 Peter 3:16 warns that Paul's letters contain *"some things hard to understand, which untaught and unstable people twist to their own destruction, as they do also the rest of the Scriptures."* So maybe Paul wrote the Corinthians a letter that was safe for them.

And maybe God preserved it for us because it is safe for us as well.

If we believe that the Word of God is inspired by the Holy Spirit, we should also believe that the providence of God was behind the circumstances that led to the New Testament letters being written and preserved in the form that they were.

We have the New Testament that God has deemed best for us to have. The 1 Corinthians in our Bible is the 1 Corinthians that He decided we needed. What does that say about us?

In John 16:12, Jesus said to His disciples, *"I still have many things to say to you, but you cannot bear them now."* We must always ask ourselves if the Lord has more to say to us than we are able to bear at the present moment.

Paul told the Corinthians that, at first, he had fed them with milk, not solid food. So, does the letter of 1 Corinthians still contain only milk? Clearly not. Paul was pulling them up to a new level, writing them a letter that they could grow into. He said later in the letter, when talking about idolatry, *"I speak as to wise men; judge for yourselves what I say"* (1 Corinthians 10:15). He was not just feeding babies, but he was challenging them to digest some mature ideas.

Besides, all of God's word will be meat to us if we take the time to chew on it.

2 Timothy 3:14-17 says, *"But you must continue in the things which you have learned and been assured of, knowing from whom you have learned them, and that from childhood you have known the Holy Scriptures, which are able to make you wise for salvation through faith which is in Christ Jesus. All Scripture is given by inspiration of God, and is profitable for doctrine, for reproof, for correction, for instruction in righteousness, that the man of God may be complete, thoroughly equipped for every good work."*

The same Scriptures that nourished Timothy as a child would train and equip him as a mature man of God. They were milk to him when he needed milk. They would be meat when he needed meat.

Lesson #18: The Word of God Speaks to Us at Our Level of Maturity and, at the Same Time, Challenges Us to Grow

Lesson #19:

God's Servants Work Together and Individually at the Same Time

Who then is Paul, and who is Apollos, but ministers through whom you believed, as the Lord gave to each one? I planted, Apollos watered, but God gave the increase. So then neither he who plants is anything, nor he who waters, but God who gives the increase. Now he who plants and he who waters are one, and each one will receive his own reward according to his own labor.

1 Corinthians 3:5-8

Paul now directly addresses the problem that he had raised at the beginning of the letter. The Corinthians were dividing into factions named after different ministers.

The ministers themselves had nothing to do with this. Paul made it clear that these ministers recognized no such division. He and Apollos, for example, did different kinds of work (planting and watering) but were on the same team. Paul put it in even stronger terms than that, saying, *"he who plants and he who waters are one"*.

Nevertheless, he finishes that sentence by saying, *"and each one will receive his own reward according to his own labor."*

These two ideas create a sharp contrast. These men are united together in their work, but they labor and are rewarded separately and individually.

This contrast appears to be intentional, for Paul said something similar in Galatians 6:2-5. *"Bear one another's burdens, and so fulfill the law of Christ. For if anyone thinks himself to be something, when he is nothing, he deceives himself. But let each one examine his own work, and then he will have rejoicing in himself alone, and not in another. For each one shall bear his own load."*

You must bear one another's burdens but remember that each will bear his own load.

There is a tension built in to both of these passages. This tension reflects two of fallen humanity's basic instincts: to divide and to unite. To both of these instincts the word of God says a clear "No!"

You could say that fallen humanity's instinct to divide manifested itself almost immediately after Adam and Eve sinned, when Adam tried to defend himself before God by saying, *"The woman whom You gave to be with me, she gave me of the tree, and I ate"* (Genesis 3:12).

This dividing instinct was more obvious when Cain killed Abel. When God asked him where Abel was, he said, "am I my brother's keeper?" Cain then followed this separating instinct to its logical conclusion, going away from the presence of the Lord (Genesis 4:9,16).

We saw in the beginning of our study (Lesson #2) that Cain built a city (which he named after his son, Enoch). This reflected fallen man's instinct to unite. After Cain had separated himself from his parents and from the presence of the Lord, he sought to unite men together around himself.

Later in Genesis, we are told about the tower of Babel. This was an epic attempt at uniting all of mankind, and it almost succeeded. God knew that this unity would have given them incredible power. *"Nothing that they propose to do will be withheld from them,"* He said (Genesis 11:6).

God then abruptly put an end to their project. He obviously did not have much confidence in what they would do with their power.

These two instincts—to divide and to unite—have continued to drive mankind throughout history. Although they seem to be in contrast with one another, the love of self is their common motivation.

Envy, pride, and selfishness tempt us to divide from one another. The word of the cross says, "No!"

Fear and insecurity tempt us to unite under the banner of man and seek safety in numbers. The word of the cross says, "No!"

Don't blame the gospel for the apparent contradiction, and don't blame the apostle Paul. Blame sinners.

God must say two different things to us, even if it is in the same sentence. He must say to us, "Yes, you are your brother's keeper; and yes, you will stand before God one day and your brother will not be there to help you."

Lesson #19: God's Servants Work Together and Individually at the Same Time

Lesson #20:

Jesus Christ Is the Only Lasting Foundation on Which We Can Build Our Lives

For we are God's fellow workers; you are God's field, you are God's building. According to the grace of God which was given to me, as a wise master builder I have laid the foundation, and another builds on it. But let each one take heed how he builds on it. For no other foundation can anyone lay than that which is laid, which is Jesus Christ.

1 Corinthians 3:9-11

The first city we see in the Bible was built by Cain. The last city we see in the Bible is built by God. Cain's city has already vanished without a trace. God's city will remain forever; it will be the *only* city.

So, the *idea* of building a city is not wrong in itself. The problem was Cain's motivation. It was what he wanted to do with the power of a people organized together.

The problem with every city built by man is the foundation. We are not talking now about physical cities with physical foundations, we are following along with Paul's metaphor. The foundation of every city built by man is in the heart of man, and that is where the problem lies.

Abraham was from Ur of the Chaldeans, perhaps the greatest city of his day. He left there and followed the call of God. Hebrews 11:8-10 describes Abraham's calling: *"By faith Abraham obeyed when he was called to go out to the place which he would receive as an inheritance. And he went out, not knowing where he was going. By faith he dwelt in the land of promise as in a foreign country, dwelling in tents with Isaac and Jacob, the heirs with him of the same promise; for he waited for the city which has foundations, whose builder and maker is God."*

By waiting for a city with foundations, Abraham was demonstrating that the city he had come from had no foundation. Hebrews does not say he was waiting for a city with *better* foundations, but one with *foundations*.

Once we have seen that the wisdom of this age is coming to nothing, we will understand that anything built on the wisdom of this age has zero solid foundational strength.

A true foundation must be laid before anything lasting can be built, and the foundation must be laid in a person's heart. The best way to be sure that you are building on the true foundation is to make sure that the same foundation has already been firmly laid in your own heart.

Hebrews 11:13-16 goes on to describe Abraham and his fellow believers: *"These all died in faith, not having received the promises, but having seen them afar off were assured of them, embraced them and confessed that they were strangers and pilgrims on the earth. For those who say such things declare plainly that they seek a homeland. And truly if they had called to mind that country from which they had come out, they would have had opportunity to return. But now they desire a better, that is, a heavenly country. Therefore God is not ashamed to be called their God, for He has prepared a city for them."*

To live by the apparent foolishness of Jesus Christ and Him crucified, and to build on that foundation, is to make a clean break with the ways of the world. Paul put this in the strongest of terms in Galatians 6:14, saying, *"God forbid that I should boast except in the cross of our Lord Jesus Christ, by whom the world has been crucified to me, and I to the world."*

This is not only a one-time experience. It is something that gets tested every day. Abraham left Ur of the Chaldeans at one point in his life. Every day after that, in his heart, he had to leave it behind. There was a comfortable life waiting for him that he could have gone back to at any time.

The passage from Hebrews, quoted above, says this about Abraham and his fellow faith-sojourners: *"And truly if they had called to mind that country from which they had come out, they would have had opportunity to return."*

Of course *"they would have had opportunity to return."* There is always the opportunity to return. The world will always take you back. It never stops calling you, offering comfort and convenience.

Now, comfort and convenience are not necessarily bad. They can be blessings from God. But they often arrive with a third companion: compromise. These three things—comfort, convenience, and compromise—often travel together, and it is that third thing that causes trouble.

It is compromise that pulls you back to the city of man. And if it can do so gradually, without you being aware of it, it will.

Don't let this happen. The city of man is a city without foundations. It is built on lies. God has built His city on the only true and lasting foundation.

Lesson #20: Jesus Christ Is the Only Lasting Foundation on Which We Can Build Our Lives

Lesson #21:

Building on the Wrong Foundation Leads to Strife and Envy

Now if anyone builds on this foundation with gold, silver, precious stones, wood, hay, straw, each one's work will become clear; for the Day will declare it, because it will be revealed by fire; and the fire will test each one's work, of what sort it is.

1 Corinthians 3:12-13

Here is a promise that God Himself will test every work that is built on His one true foundation. God is jealous for the purity of His church.

He is not jealous, however, for works which men build for themselves. He has no obligation to protect any work not built on the foundation of Jesus Christ and Him crucified. When men build their own works on their own foundations, they will have to be jealous for them with their own jealousy.

Paul had a policy of not building on a spiritual foundation that had been laid by someone else, as he explained in Romans 15:20-21 (see also 2 Corinthians 10:13-17). This was because of Paul's own apostolic calling. He followed this rule for himself, but in general, he was not opposed to the idea of a minister building on a foundation laid by another. Neither was he against other ministers building on the foundation he had laid.

Considering how hard Paul had worked and how much he had sacrificed in order to establish the church in Corinth, he was remarkably tolerant of other ministers building on his foundation. He left an immature, vulnerable group of converts, knowing that other people would come there and preach, sometimes with a different style or emphasis than Paul, and sometimes with a different gospel!

Paul could not stop this from happening. As far as a false gospel was concerned, he had to hope that the church would recognize and reject it. When it came to fellow ministers with different styles visiting the church, it appears that he encouraged it.

Paul wrote 1 Corinthians 1-4, in part, because the people were dividing over loyalty to different ministers. Because of the trouble this caused, Paul could have thought to himself, "Maybe it's better that they just hear from one minister until they are more mature. Maybe the variety is not good for them now."

Instead, he took a different approach. Look, for example, at what he said at the end of the letter (1 Corinthians 16:12): *"Now concerning our brother Apollos, I strongly urged him to come to you with the brethren ..."* Even though they had been dividing from one another, saying "I am of Paul," and "I am of Apollos," Paul still thought another visit from Apollos would be good for them.

Paul trusted Apollos. As far as the gospel being preached by ministers he didn't trust, Philippians 1:15-18 reveals something of his attitude toward that: *"Some indeed preach Christ even from envy and strife, and some also from goodwill: The former preach Christ from selfish ambition, not sincerely, supposing to add affliction to my chains; but the latter out of love, knowing that I am appointed for the defense of the gospel. What then? Only that in every way, whether in pretense or in truth, Christ is preached; and in this I rejoice, yes, and will rejoice."*

Paul did not put up with a false gospel being preached. He condemned it and rebuked any church that would tolerate it. (See, for example Galatians 1:8-9 and 2 Corinthians 11:3-4.) But that wasn't the issue he was addressing in Philippians. Look at what he said there: some people were preaching Christ from envy, strife, and selfish ambition. The problem was not their message, it was their motives.

Paul rejoiced that Christ was preached even by men with impure motives. He really had no choice. He couldn't judge the motives of others even if he wanted to. The message, yes; the motives, no.

As we saw in the previous lesson, Paul said, *"let each one take heed how he builds."* This is a matter that each minister must attend to himself, and it involves a person's motives. It's about *how* he builds.

The human heart is complex. In reality, someone can preach Christ motivated by 90% love and goodwill, yet still have some remnants of envy and selfish ambition.

This is not a matter of heresy or blatant sin, but of the motives of a person's heart. This is a matter for the Lord to judge. No individual can rightly judge their own motives.

We must examine our motives as best we can and then trust the Lord to judge perfectly. As we will see later in our study, although each one must take care how he builds, he ultimately needs the Lord to judge his work as he goes along (Lesson #26).

In the end, what sort of work is being built on the foundation will depend on the heart of the worker. And the heart of each worker can only be perfectly understood by the Lord. These are matters that Jesus is good at dealing with. He is the master of the human heart and a worthy judge. He can be trusted to judge His ministers and to build His church.

If Paul had built the church in Corinth on a foundation of his own devising, it is doubtful that he would have been able to leave and stay away for so long, knowing that other ministers would be passing through and preaching to the people, and that he had no control over what they would say.

Paul said, in 2 Corinthians 11:2, *"I am jealous for you with a godly jealously."* He could say that because he had built on the right foundation. His concern was that the Corinthians would stay loyal to Christ, not to Paul. Because he had built for the Lord, he could trust the Lord to judge the work that others would do after he left Corinth.

If someone builds on any other foundation than Jesus Christ, they will also be jealous for the church. But it will not be a godly jealousy. It will be very human.

As we saw in the beginning of our study (Lesson #3), envy must be guarded against from the beginning. It is much easier to prevent it from taking root than it is to uproot it. The best way to do this is to make sure that you are building on the only true and lasting foundation. This will result in godly jealousy, and godly jealousy, when it burns hot enough, leaves no room for human jealousy.

Lesson #21: Building on the Wrong Foundation Leads to Strife and Envy

Lesson #22:

Either We Will Allow God to Keep Us from Self-Deception or Jesus Will Cleanse His Work of the Mess We Make

If anyone's work which he has built on it endures, he will receive a reward. If anyone's work is burned, he will suffer loss; but he himself will be saved, yet so as through fire.

1 Corinthians 3:14-15

We don't live in a world of black and white, where the sinners sin and the saints do nothing but good and holy deeds. A lot of the pain in the world is caused by Christians, sometimes by ministers of the gospel, and sometimes by ministers who think they are doing good, or at least don't see the harm they are causing.

We need Jesus to judge. No one else is worthy or qualified. Some of this judgment He does now, by the Holy Spirit and the Word of God. Complete judgment, however, will have to wait for the Day of testing and fire that Paul is describing in these verses.

On that Day, some will discover that the work that they thought would endure will be burned. How can this happen? How could someone build so wrongly that they suffer loss instead of the reward they were expecting? More importantly, how can this be avoided?

Paul would go on to say, a few verses later, *"Let no one deceive himself."* There are many kinds of self-deceptions that can take root in a well-meaning person's heart. Let us consider three. These three are common not only to those who do the work of the gospel, but also to anyone who wants to live a life faithful to God.

First, people deceive themselves by secret motives. Their own selfish ambitions go undetected.

We saw in the previous lesson that Paul rejoiced that Christ was preached, even if He was preached by men with selfish motives (Philippians 1:15-18). Paul understood that, although he could evaluate their message and their conduct, he could not judge their motives.

That does not mean, however, that motives will not be judged. Jesus will judge them on that coming Day. But also, as we will see later in our study (Lesson #26), He will begin to judge our motives for us even now, if we seek His judgment and submit to it.

This is what we should desire. We should want Him to start judging us now, as much as possible. We should understand that when selfish motives hide themselves from us, they lead us into greater self-deception.

The second deception for us to consider is the idea that the end justifies the means.

It may not be articulated in these exact words. It may not be well articulated at all. It may be a simple thought from within by which God's servant reassures his or her own conscience. But if this seed of a thought were given words, it may say this: "I have to do it this way to get results. Anyway, it's for the kingdom of God, it's not for me."

This is a great delusion. The end will not justify the means. The fire that Paul is talking about will make sure of that.

How you go about getting your message heard is part of the message. The purity of the gospel will not cleanse ethically shady tactics. On the contrary, the methods with reflect unfairly on the message.

Paul avoided this trap, and this was a point of pride for him—a healthy kind of boasting. He said, in 2 Corinthians 1:12, *"For our boasting is this: the testimony of our conscience that we conducted ourselves in the world in simplicity and godly sincerity, not with fleshly wisdom but by the grace of God, and more abundantly toward you."*

The third deception is another one that usually goes unarticulated, but it could be expressed this way: "I will be evaluated in terms of what everybody else around me is doing."

As we have considered in an earlier lesson (#19), fallen humanity tends to seek safety in numbers. This is one reason why people deceive themselves in this way. It seems safe to do something if a lot of people are already doing it.

The other reason for this kind of self-deception is the other tendency of fallen humanity: to turn against one another. As we have seen, Adam's first reaction after sinning was to point to Eve and say that he was influenced by her, as if this might excuse him from his own actions. It didn't work then, it doesn't work now, and it won't work on Judgment Day.

Lesson #22: Either We Will Allow God to Keep Us from Self-Deception or Jesus Will Cleanse His Work of the Mess We Make

Lesson #23:

To Be the Church of God Is a Gift of Grace Not to Be Taken Lightly

Do you not know that you are the temple of God and that the Spirit of God dwells in you? If anyone defiles the temple of God, God will destroy him. For the temple of God is holy, which temple you are.

1 Corinthians 3:16-17

Paul reminds the Corinthians that they are the temple of God—not that they *will be* if they get their act together, but that they *are*. As serious as the problems were in Corinth, Paul affirmed that they were, already, the holy temple of God.

Paul rebuked and corrected throughout his letters, dealing with all kinds of sins and manifestations of the flesh. Yet he did it without once saying a negative word about the church *as the church*.

It is not just Paul who did this. All the writers of the New Testament used the word *church* in a positive context only.

Paul wrote to the *"churches of Galatia,"* but when it was time to rebuke them, he said, *"O foolish Galatians,"* not, "O foolish churches." (Galatians 1:2,3:1)

Paul rebuked the Corinthians for their lack of wisdom: *"I say this to your shame. Is it so, that there is not a wise man among you, not even one, who will be able to judge between his brethren?"* (1 Corinthians 6:5)

Yet he did not say "you are not a wise church."

If this happened once or twice you could say it was a coincidence. But all throughout the New Testament, when the dirty work of dealing with sin and immaturity among believers is done, the word *church* is kept sparklingly clean.

The word *church* was not even a special word. It was an everyday word that meant *assembly*. But when it referred to the church of God, it was a holy word. All the immaturity and sin of the members of the churches could not corrupt it.

The closest thing I have found to Paul using the word *church* in a negative context is 1 Corinthians 11:17-18: *"Now in giving these instructions I do not praise you, since you come together not for the better but for the worse. For first of all, when you come together as a church, I hear that there are divisions among you, and in part I believe it."*

He doesn't quite say the church is bad, but he does say that they are coming together as a church in a detrimental way.

But even then, look what he goes on to say: *"For there must also be factions among you, that those who are approved may be recognized among you. Therefore when you come together in one place, it is not to eat the Lord's Supper. For in eating, each one takes his own supper ahead of others; and one is hungry and another is drunk. What! Do you not have houses to eat and drink in? Or do you despise the church of God and shame those who have nothing? What shall I say to you? Shall I praise you in this? I do not praise you."* (1 Corinthians 11:19-22)

One of the reasons he gives for their problems is that they *"despise the church of God."* It was the lack of respect and honor for the church that made their coming together detrimental.

There is no carnal church in Paul's letters. There are carnal Corinthians who come together and yet have no respect for the holiness of God's church.

There is no foolish church. There are foolish Galatians who come together as a church but do not realize the wisdom that God has given to His church.

But the people *are* the church, so what difference does it make?

Yes, the people are the church. As Peter said, they are living stones being built into a holy temple (1 Peter 2:4-5, see also Ephesians 2:19-22). But a temple is more than a collection of stones. It is something in and of itself.

The church is also spoken of as the body of Christ, but a body is more than a collection of body parts.

Something happens when the church meets, or even when the church doesn't meet. Something happens when the church is looked at from a heavenly perspective. Perhaps a suitable word for what is happening is *gestalt,* the German word that refers to something that is made of many parts and yet is somehow more than, or different from, the combination of its parts.

Perhaps it is safer just to call it a *mystery,* as Paul himself referred to the great mystery of Christ and the church (Ephesians 5:32).

You may still argue that Paul could just as easily have said, "you foolish churches" instead of "you foolish Galatians." I can't prove you wrong. But the sense I get as I read the New Testament is that a sentence like that would never have come out of his mouth.

It seems that the word *church* never left the apostles' lips without a sense of deep respect. The New Testament leaves the impression that they uttered that word ever mindful that they were talking about Jesus' wife—and He was listening!

Then we come to Jesus Himself in the book of Revelation. If anyone has the right to rebuke the church as the church, it's Him. And He does rebuke. He has strong words of warning for some of the seven churches in Revelation 2-3.

But look closely at what He says. When rebuking the believers in Ephesus for losing their first love, He warns them, saying, *"Remember therefore from where you have fallen; repent and do the first works, or else I will come to you quickly and remove your lampstand from its place— unless you repent."* (Revelation 2:5)

What is the lampstand that He is threatening to remove? He had already explained: *"the seven lampstands which you saw are the seven churches."* (Revelation 1:20)

Jesus rebukes the believers that make up the church and warns them that they are going to stop being a church. Now, if He is threatening to take away His church, then He is not exactly rebuking the church as a church, but as a group of believers to whom has been given the mysterious gift of being the church.

The Ephesians could have continued to meet together after Jesus had taken their lampstand away, and they still could have called themselves a church, but they would not have been a church recognized in heaven. We humans don't just decide to be the church. It is a gift of God, not a matter of organization.

Today, our vocabulary is different. We have two different uses for the word *church*. First, we speak of the church as a human institution, as in, "That's a good church over there but that church is weak, that church is lazy, and in general, the problem with the church today is..."

This all might add up to helpful and accurate analysis, and this kind of truthful talk is necessary. But then we also want to speak of the church in another sense, as the glorious mystery that is Christ's beloved bride, and we use the same word.

Words change and the way we use them changes and we can't go back. We can't change what the word *church* means, and I don't think we should try. Nevertheless, we can still recover and maintain a healthy respect for the holy mystery that is the church. We can have reverence for this mystery in our hearts, and it should be seen in the way we talk, regardless of our exact vocabulary.

Lesson #23: To Be the Church of God Is a Gift of Grace Not to Be Taken Lightly

Lesson #24:

God Is the Author of Both Heavenly Wisdom and Earthly Wisdom

Let no one deceive himself. If anyone among you seems to be wise in this age, let him become a fool that he may become wise. For the wisdom of this world is foolishness with God. For it is written, "He catches the wise in their own craftiness"; and again, "The Lord knows the thoughts of the wise, that they are futile."

1 Corinthians 3:18-20

This sounds like the passage that Paul began his argument with back in 1 Corinthians 1:18-19 (see Lesson #4). There, he compared man's wisdom to God's and quoted the Old Testament. He does the same thing here in this passage, as he is concluding his argument. But there he spoke of God's wisdom as foolishness. Here it is man's wisdom that is foolishness.

We have seen, in our study, that the word of the cross offends man's sense of pride and self-sufficiency, insulting his supposed wisdom. Paul called this wisdom by three names: the wisdom of this world, the wisdom of this age, and the wisdom of man. In the light of this wisdom, the preaching of the cross could only be seen as foolishness.

God's wisdom is so different and so far above us that it can't be compared with human wisdom. That is why Paul went so far as to call it foolishness. He was using the terms and categories that the worldly-minded Corinthians would have used.

By arguing this way, Paul risked being misunderstood. He was comparing heavenly wisdom with worldly wisdom, and what he said needs to be understood in that context. The potential for misunderstanding lies in the fact that there is a third kind of wisdom, which could be confused with one of the other two kinds.

This third kind of wisdom is also a gift from God and it is very good. It is not mysterious or hidden. God has already given it generously to all people. In fact, God has been so generous in distributing this gift that it is sometimes called *common sense.* It is called other things as well. It includes various kinds of human intelligence. Here we will call it *earthly wisdom,* and it is not to be confused, of course, with the heavenly wisdom that is hidden in the word of the cross and revealed by the Holy Spirit.

Neither is this earthly wisdom to be confused with the worldly wisdom that Paul has been talking about in 1 Corinthians. If we were to make that mistake, we might conclude that Paul was disparaging logic and reasoning, which are part of earthly wisdom.

As we saw in an earlier lesson (#5), the gospel is not anti-intellectual. In calling people to believe the gospel, God is not asking them to turn off their brains, as if they must believe that 2 + 2 = 5, no matter what it looks like.

The gospel is an offense to *worldly wisdom,* which is really the pride and foolishness of fallen humanity. It does not violate *earthly wisdom,* however. On the contrary, by revealing worldly wisdom as the foolishness it really is, it distinguishes it from earthly wisdom, which can then be appreciated as a gift from God.

It is important to make this distinction. There are many people who have been given much earthly wisdom, yet they reject the heavenly wisdom of the gospel. When we understand, with Paul, that it is *worldly* wisdom that opposes the word of the cross, then we can benefit from the *earthly* wisdom that God has generously given to all people, believers and unbelievers alike.

The reasons why people don't believe the gospel are, from a human standpoint, many and complex. Humans are complex beings, and we don't want to put them into simplistic categories. But nobody rejects the gospel because they are too intelligent. True intelligence is not a barrier to faith. God is the giver of intelligence and all earthly wisdom, and He would not give us something that would make it harder for us to trust Him.

The Bible itself teaches both heavenly wisdom and earthly wisdom. In fact, it is the best book on earthly wisdom that there is, and some people read it only for that, and receive the benefits of earthly wisdom while rejecting the heavenly wisdom of the gospel.

The writings of Moses and Solomon, for example, are especially rich in earthly wisdom. When studied, they lead to success in earthly endeavors. The principles they contain are timeless and they work when followed, even for people who don't believe in God.

There is a difference between Moses and Solomon, however.

As we considered in an earlier lesson (#13), because Moses' job was so hard, he asked God for help, saying, "Show me your glory." He saw the glory, and there was wisdom in the glory. He received both earthly wisdom as well as prophetic insight into the hidden wisdom of the cross.

When King Solomon saw how hard his job would be, he also asked God for help. "Give me wisdom and knowledge," he said, "and an understanding mind" (see 2 Chronicles 1:7-12 and 1 Kings 3:9-12). He received wisdom and knowledge. It helped him rule the kingdom and become amazingly wealthy.

Solomon's wisdom, however, was more of the practical, earthly kind than the prophetic, spiritual kind. He had his prophetic moments as well. He also experienced the glory of God, seeing the cloud of glory fill the temple, for example. But he was no Moses.

For all the earthly wisdom that Solomon had been blessed with, he seemed reluctant to give up on worldly wisdom, and this limited his spiritual vision.

Using earthly wisdom, he achieved remarkable wealth and peace even while disobeying God. (Later, however, the nation of Israel paid a heavy price for this disobedience.)

Solomon was world-famous for his wisdom, yet he also made some astonishingly foolish mistakes. He collected wives and horses against the clear command of God (the horses were for military purposes).

Despite this disobedience, God did not take back His gift of wisdom. Solomon remained wise, and at the end of his life, his earthly wisdom gave him insight (or hindsight) into the foolishness of the things that his worldly wisdom had led him to do.

Solomon got what he asked for. He asked for wisdom and knowledge, and he became the wisest, most knowledgeable man of his generation. But maybe he should have asked to see God's glory instead.

Solomon asked for earthly wisdom and he got it. Moses asked only to see God's glory and he saw it, and along with it, he got wisdom, knowledge, understanding, and much more.

Lesson #24: God Is the Author of Both Heavenly Wisdom and Earthly Wisdom

Lesson #25:

When You Can Do Without All Things For Christ, You Can Do All Things Through Christ

Therefore let no one boast in men. For all things are yours: whether Paul or Apollos or Cephas, or the world or life or death, or things present or things to come—all are yours. And you are Christ's, and Christ is God's.

1 Corinthians 3:21-23

The Corinthians' boasting in men was, at its root, boasting in themselves. They were boasting in their own ability to choose the best men to follow. Ultimately, they were more concerned about their own reputations than about the truth.

The Corinthians were eager to associate themselves with the particular gifts they saw in these ministers. Apollos was eloquent, Paul was educated, Peter was powerful. There was no need, however, to choose just one of these gifts when all of them had been given to the church already.

The Corinthians did not realize what God had given them. They were acting from what businessman and educator Stephen Covey called the Scarcity Mentality.

This is the idea that there is a limited supply of something—success, for example—and if someone else succeeds it means there is less success available for you.

This is a detrimental way of thinking in the world of business, when it comes to things like opportunity, wealth, and success. The Corinthians, however, had this mentality regarding the truth of the gospel and the unlimited Spirit of God. In this context, the Scarcity Mentality is not only detrimental, but truly absurd. Nevertheless, it is also very common, even to this day.

Covey also described what he called the Abundance Mentality. This is the recognition that somebody else's gain is not your loss, and that there is always more opportunity and success available.

The Abundance Mentality is the mindset that fits the truth of the gospel, and it is seen in these words of Paul: *"All things are yours."*

If the Corinthians saw something that they admired in the ministry of Apollos, there was no need for them to put their stamp of boasting on it. God had already given it to them.

All things were theirs as long as they had the right mindset. If they became covetous and self-centered, nothing was theirs. Everything depended on their perspective. They were called to look at the world with something even greater than an abundance mentality.

If I were to say, "All things are *available* to me," that is an example of abundance thinking. If I were to say, "All things are *mine*," that's either misguided, crazy, or gospel-driven abundance thinking.

Paul went further. He didn't say, "all things are mine," he said, "all things are *yours*." This is gospel-driven abundance thinking expressed with a servant's heart.

In the verses coming after this passage, Paul would explain that he himself at times didn't get enough to eat. He would even describe himself as *"poorly-clothed, beaten, and homeless"* (1 Corinthians 4:11).

When you can be suffering the things Paul suffered and look at a group of competitive, selfish, immature Christians and say, "all things are yours," that's more than an abundance mindset. It's a redemption mindset combined with a servant mindset, an apostolic mindset, and more.

Actually, it's simpler than that. It's the mind of Christ.

Paul did, in another place, claim to possess everything himself, but in the same breath he said he owned nothing. He described himself as *"having nothing, yet possessing all things"* (2 Corinthians 6:10).

If I told you that it's not about what you have, but what you possess, and that you can possess what you don't have, you wouldn't take me seriously. I don't blame you. Coming from me it sounds like a silly and meaningless play on words.

But it was Paul who made that distinction, not me. He lived it. He learned it. He earned the right to say it.

Paul also explained, in Philippians 4:11-13, that he had learned contentment: *"I have learned in whatever state I am, to be content: I know how to be abased, and I know how to abound. Everywhere and in all things I have learned both to be full and to be hungry, both to abound and to suffer need. I can do all things through Christ who strengthens me."*

There is the gift of contentment and then there is the discipline. This is the discipline. This is something Paul had learned over time. As he learned this lesson, he learned what was essential and what wasn't, and he learned the difference between having and possessing.

We can all learn the same lesson, and God wants us to. You might not have to suffer the same things Paul suffered to learn the same lesson. A lot of his lack was the result of what it was like to travel in those days, and Paul traveled a lot.

Regardless of how it happens, though, you can learn the same lesson of contentment. We all can.

Once we have learned it like Paul had learned it, then we can better understand the context of Paul's words in Philippians 4:13: *"I can do all things through Christ who strengthens me."*

Paul transcended his own abilities when he transcended his own needs. We can do the same, and like Paul, we can learn this lesson.

Lesson #25: When You Can Do *Without* All Things *For* Christ, You Can *Do* All Things *Through* Christ

Lesson #26:

To Live in God's Presence Is to Live with a Perfect, All-Knowing Judge

Let a man so consider us, as servants of Christ and stewards of the mysteries of God. Moreover it is required in stewards that one be found faithful. But with me it is a very small thing that I should be judged by you or by a human court. In fact, I do not even judge myself. For I know of nothing against myself, yet I am not justified by this; but He who judges me is the Lord. Therefore judge nothing before the time, until the Lord comes, who will both bring to light the hidden things of darkness and reveal the counsels of the hearts. Then each one's praise will come from God.

1 Corinthians 4:1-5

Every time the New Testament speaks of judging, we must pay close attention to the context in order to know what kind of judging is in view, for there is more than one way to judge.

Here Paul says, *"I do not even judge myself."* Later, in 1 Corinthians 11:31, he says, *"But if we would judge ourselves, we would not be judged."*

In fact, 1 Corinthians has many lessons to teach about judging, both the right kind and the wrong kind.

The Corinthians were engaged in the wrong kind of judging and had neglected the right kind. They were dividing over which preacher they would prefer to listen to. Meanwhile, a man was sleeping with his father's wife and went undisciplined.

In the passage above, Paul is talking about the ultimate motives of his heart. These were hidden even from him.

Jeremiah 17:9-10 teaches that it is beyond human beings to fully comprehend their own motives:

"The heart is deceitful above all things,
And desperately wicked;
Who can know it?
I, the Lord, search the heart,
I test the mind,
Even to give every man according to his ways,
According to the fruit of his doings."

When it came to the deepest counsels of his heart, Paul didn't judge himself because he *couldn't* judge himself. What he *could* do, however, was to stay close to the Judge.

In the future, Jesus will render His judgment on all things. That same Jesus is present with us in the Spirit. God's presence always results in judgment, one way or another, because judgment is part of God's nature.

There is a Day coming in which the Lord *"will both bring to light the hidden things of darkness and reveal the counsels of the hearts."* That Day will surely come, but Paul speaks in the present tense when he refers to Christ as *"He who judges me."*

If we really believe that we will be perfectly judged in the future, we should want as much of that judgment to happen today, while we still have time to change, rather than on Judgment Day, when it will be too late. You don't want there to be any surprises for you on that Day. You don't want the bad kind, anyway. Therefore, you should want God to judge you every day, as much as possible.

The good news is that God wants us to change as much as possible in this life, and He makes His judgment available to us daily. God will judge us every day if we want Him to. He will judge us directly in our conscience by His Spirit and by His Word. He will judge us by circumstances and by other people.

We must be able to discern God judging us by these means, however, and there are things that get in the way of this discernment.

In an earlier lesson (#18), we saw that Jesus said to His disciples, *"I still have many things to say to you, but you cannot bear them now"* (John 16:12). This is often true for us when it comes to receiving judgment. It doesn't have to be this way, however. His judgments don't have to be unbearable. There are things we do that make God's judgment hard for us to hear, and we can learn not to do these things.

For one thing, we will not be able to discern God's judgment if we think of it only as punishment or rejection, and never as loving correction. Hebrews 12 teaches us that discipline in this life is a sign of God's love for us, and that what we should really fear is *not* being disciplined (see Hebrews 12:3-11).

There is another thing that will keep us from discerning God's loving discipline in our lives. It is our own, deeply flawed, self-evaluation. We don't want to abandon self-judgment, but we need to know its limits.

You should do the best you can to make sure that you are doing what you do for the right reasons, but the deeper you peer into your own heart, the less reliable your own judgment becomes.

We can judge our outward behavior, and we should. For example, Paul boasted that the testimony of his conscience was that his conduct in the world had been simple and sincere (see 2 Corinthians 1:12).

We are very limited, however, at judging the motives of our own hearts, and our judgment in that area is not as clear as God's judgment. What we list as our greatest flaw might not even make it onto God's top ten list.

Jesus taught His disciples that they could pray with the confidence that God already knew their needs. They did not need to spend all their energy in prayer trying to convince God that their needs were legitimate. He instructed them in Matthew 6:7-8: *"And when you pray, do not use vain repetitions as the heathen do.*

For they think that they will be heard for their many words. Therefore do not be like them. For your Father knows the things you have need of before you ask Him." (Matthew 6:7-8)

This lesson, about approaching God as our provider, can also be applied to approaching God as our judge. Just as God already knows your needs, He already knows your motives. You don't have to spend all your time and energy in prayer explaining yourself to Him. Prayer is not meant to be a lifetime of introducing yourself to God. He already knows you. And, fortunately for you, He is already judging you.

Lesson #26: To Live in God's Presence Is to Live with a Perfect, All-Knowing Judge

Lesson #27:

The Gospel Gives Us the Mental Framework to Solve Every Kind of Problem That We Will Face in Church Life

Now these things, brethren, I have figuratively transferred to myself and Apollos for your sakes, that you may learn in us not to think beyond what is written, that none of you may be puffed up on behalf of one against the other. For who makes you differ from another? And what do you have that you did not receive? Now if you did indeed receive it, why do you boast as if you had not received it?

1 Corinthians 4:6-7

Paul exposes the foolishness of the Corinthians' thinking by asking them some simple questions. What do they have that they did not receive? Nothing. Of course they can't claim any ability that has been generated from themselves. Everything they have is a gift from God. Paul and Apollos, likewise, only have what God has given them.

Paul then indicates that their problem was caused by what he calls "thinking beyond what is written." Their thinking didn't conform to Scripture and so, by default, it conformed to the foolishness of worldly wisdom.

The mind of Christ is not a replacement for Scripture. The mind of Christ is the revelation of true scriptural thinking, and will never contradict what is written, just as Jesus never contradicted Scripture throughout His earthly ministry.

To be told not to think beyond what is written is not a limitation on the imagination. On the contrary, the biblical witness to the mind of Christ sets our minds free. The truth always sets free. It is deception that limits and controls us. Not to think beyond what is written means not to fall into the bondage of deception.

The Corinthians had not been following this advice about thinking scripturally. The result was that, instead of not thinking beyond what was written, they didn't think beyond what was preached. It was this kind of thinking that put great restrictions on their imagination.

No doubt, Paul and Apollos were both great preachers in their own different ways. But they were simply men, and if we only listen to one man's explanation of the truth, even if it is accurate, it will be limiting.

The Bible itself was written by many different kinds of men over many years. Each Old Testament prophet and each New Testament apostle had a different perspective and emphasis. This is not a weakness but a strength.

When Paul warns them *"not to think beyond what is written,"* some scholars understand him to be referring to the things that he had already said in 1 Corinthians, rather than to Scripture in general. Even if this is the case, it doesn't change the force of what Paul is saying. It would mean that he is pointing to his own teaching as a good example of scriptural thinking.

This is the way that Paul normally taught in his letters, not only quoting Scripture, but also revealing his own thought process. Christian living requires us to think through difficult issues, and Paul set himself forth as an example of this.

Of course, there are some plain and clear issues of right and wrong, concerning which the commands in the Bible are simple and direct. But even in those cases, God wants us to see with Him *why* certain sins are wrong and why He forbids them.

In addition to simple matters of right and wrong, there are also bound to be complex questions that require thoughtful consideration. When the Corinthians were faced with these kinds of issues, Paul walked them through the problem, thought by scriptural thought.

A good example of this is 1 Corinthians 8-10, in which Paul addressed a question about whether they could eat food that had come from animals that had been offered to idols.

He could have said, "Don't do it because I'm an apostle and I said so!" Instead, he walked them through his reasoning, and he started by demonstrating that he could sympathize with both sides of the issue. He looked at the issue from each perspective while always keeping in mind what was most important.

Paul even seemed to stray from the subject completely in 1 Corinthians 9, addressing some other complaints that had been made about his ministry. This was not a distraction, however. Paul not only defended his apostolic ministry, but he used that defense as an opportunity to give himself as an example of how the Corinthians should be thinking and behaving. Even while defending his ministry, he was still teaching the Corinthians how to think biblically.

Then, when we get to 1 Corinthians 10, we find that he hasn't forgotten the subject at all. He returns to the issue of idolatry and summarizes his argument with an appeal to imitate him in doing all things for the sake of the gospel.

Because Paul taught this way, instead of just issuing orders, his writing has continued to be helpful to Christians throughout the centuries. He dealt with issues that were specific to first-century Christians living in the Roman Empire. Nevertheless, because he revealed his approach to biblical problem-solving, we can solve our own, very different problems by learning from his example.

Lesson #27: The Gospel Gives Us the Mental Framework to Solve Every Kind of Problem That We Will Face in Church Life

Lesson #28:

Biblical Leadership Doesn't Accept the World's Standards, but Lives by and Sets Forth God's Standards

You are already full! You are already rich! You have reigned as kings without us—and indeed I could wish you did reign, that we also might reign with you! For I think that God has displayed us, the apostles, last, as men condemned to death; for we have been made a spectacle to the world, both to angels and to men. We are fools for Christ's sake, but you are wise in Christ! We are weak, but you are strong! You are distinguished, but we are dishonored! To the present hour we both hunger and thirst, and we are poorly clothed, and beaten, and homeless. And we labor, working with our own hands. Being reviled, we bless; being persecuted, we endure; being defamed, we entreat. We have been made as the filth of the world, the offscouring of all things until now.

1 Corinthians 4:8-13

Hopefully, by this point the Corinthians clearly understood that when Paul told them that they were wise and strong in Christ, he meant that they were really only wise and strong by worldly standards, and that they had been deceiving themselves into thinking that their wisdom was in Christ. In the eyes of heaven, they were still foolish and weak, and they were not yet reigning as they were called to.

Paul and his fellow apostles, on the other hand, were indeed wise and strong in Christ, but they looked foolish and weak in the eyes of the world.

Every culture creates standards for what winning looks like, and the apostles didn't fit that mold. But by holding fast to the hidden wisdom of the cross and living by the mind of Christ, they were setting the true standard for the church to follow, rather than submitting to the standards that the world tried to impose upon them. That's what leadership does, and that's why God put them on display for all the world to see.

Paul described himself as a *spectacle*. It may have looked like God was putting the apostles on the world stage to be mocked. However, it was not to entertain the world that God displayed the apostles, but to teach it.

The church will always need leaders to model what following Christ looks like, to keep believers from being conformed to the standards of the world. This kind of leadership entails suffering and often persecution. In Colossians 1:24, Paul refers to this need for leadership, and how God supplied the need through his ministry: *"I now rejoice in my sufferings for you, and fill up in my flesh what is lacking in the afflictions of Christ, for the sake of His body, which is the church..."*

The afflictions of Christ lack nothing in terms of their power to save. Christ suffered to the uttermost and is able to save to the uttermost. The redemption that Christ accomplished is indeed a perfect, finished work.

What was *"lacking in the afflictions of Christ"* was an army of messengers who would embody the very message that they announced. The finished work of Christ still needed to be communicated to the world and to the church.

Paul and his fellow apostles were not unique in the things they suffered. A lot of people were suffering similar things every day. What made the apostles a spectacle to the world was *why* they suffered, or perhaps more accurately, why they didn't try to avoid it. It would have been easy to avoid. All their suffering would have stopped if they had just kept their mouths shut.

Paul wasn't complaining that he was a spectacle to the world. He understood it to be part of his job, and part of the sufferings in which he rejoiced.

The apostles were set forth as an example to the church and a puzzle to the rest of the world. In a world of winners and losers, they seemed to be playing by a different set of rules.

As we saw in a previous lesson (#17), those who are spiritual are *"rightly judged by no one"* (1 Corinthians 2:15). They can't be figured out, but they can't be ignored either. They are as mesmerizing as they are strange.

They are also hated. They are despised by the world just as Jesus was. This is to be expected. Christ-like leaders will be treated like Christ was treated. What is tragic and unnecessary, however, is that such leaders are often overlooked by Christians when they should be honored instead.

Remember what we saw in an earlier lesson (#11): If we judge the messenger by worldly standards, we will miss the glory of the message. God will give us leaders who will challenge our worldly-mindedness. Our job is to recognize and honor them, and as we will see in the next lesson, to imitate them.

Lesson #28: Biblical Leadership Doesn't Accept the World's Standards, but Lives by and Sets Forth God's Standards

Lesson #29:

If We Imitate Spiritual Fathers, They Will Lead Us to Christ

I do not write these things to shame you, but as my beloved children I warn you. For though you might have ten thousand instructors in Christ, yet you do not have many fathers; for in Christ Jesus I have begotten you through the gospel. Therefore I urge you, imitate me. For this reason I have sent Timothy to you, who is my beloved and faithful son in the Lord, who will remind you of my ways in Christ, as I teach everywhere in every church.

1 Corinthians 4:14-17

Paul closes his argument with one final appeal: *"I urge you, imitate me."*

This is a bold thing to say in light of the problem he was addressing, the problem of people saying, "I am of Paul" and "I am of Apollos." Identifying with specific leaders was a source of division for the Corinthians.

The solution, however, was not for them to stop following leaders. So, Paul says, "Imitate me."

They were not to say, "I am of Paul," but they were to *imitate* Paul as children imitate their father. Therefore, they needed to make a distinction between identifying with a leader the wrong way and imitating him the right way.

Let us recall the second lesson in our study. There we saw that the goal of a servant of God is to disappear, but to disappear the hard way and not the easy way. The easy way is to hide from taking responsibility for your words, to put a safe distance between you and the people you are serving.

The hard way is to be available and accessible, yet always be pointing beyond yourself to Christ.

As we have just seen in the previous lesson, one reason this way is so hard is because it involves sharing in the sufferings of Christ. Commitment to Christ brings suffering, although it might not result in the same degree of suffering that Paul described as happening to him. Then again, there is no guarantee that it won't.

Disappearing the hard way and not the easy way is a lesson about service, therefore it is a lesson about leadership. The same lesson, however, can be looked at from the point of view of a follower. In fact, it is learned first as a follower. A leader who has never been a follower is not a leader but a bully.

Usually, when a Christian says that a certain person led them to Christ, they mean that person was instrumental in their initial conversion. However, being led to Christ does not end at conversion. You need people to lead you to Christ, not only as a matter of initial conversion, but also as a matter of daily discipleship. Therefore, you need to learn how to follow people, and to follow them in such a way that you are actually following Christ.

Part of following is imitating. As a follower, you can and should learn to imitate other people, and to do so in a way that leads you closer to Christ, not further away from Him. There is a way to respect and honor other people that will increase your reverence for Christ. That is the way to learn effectively from leaders.

Timothy imitated his spiritual father, Paul, but he did not idolize him. Therefore, Timothy was useful to Paul, and became more useful as time went by.

Imitation is temporary. I am convinced that, as he grew, Timothy became less like Paul and more like himself; he developed his own style over time. I am convinced of this because this is what happens with sons. Both spiritual and natural sons and daughters start out acting like their parents or role models, but end up becoming parents or role models themselves.

On the other hand, people who idolize other people get stuck. They don't grow. Neither do they help the people they idolize. To idolize someone is to try to put a burden on them that they were never meant to carry. You will never learn anything from an idol. You will learn from leaders, even from heroes, but not from idols.

2 Kings 2:9-13 describes how the prophet Elijah, at the end of his life, passed his ministry on to his disciple Elisha:

"And so it was, when they had crossed over, that Elijah said to Elisha, 'Ask! What may I do for you, before I am taken away from you?'

"Elisha said, 'Please let a double portion of your spirit be upon me.'

"So he said, 'You have asked a hard thing. Nevertheless, if you see me when I am taken from you, it shall be so for you; but if not, it shall not be so.' Then it happened, as they continued on and talked, that suddenly a chariot of fire appeared with horses of fire, and separated the two of them; and Elijah went up by a whirlwind into heaven.

"And Elisha saw it, and he cried out, 'My father, my father, the chariot of Israel and its horsemen!' So he saw him no more. And he took hold of his own clothes and tore them into two pieces. He also took up the mantle of Elijah that had fallen from him, and went back and stood by the bank of the Jordan."

Elijah left this world in a most dramatic fashion, which was fitting considering how he lived in the world. It was not enough, however, for Elisha to see the chariot of fire and the whirlwind. Elijah said to him, "If you see *me* when I am taken from you, it shall be so for you."

As Elisha followed Elijah during his lifetime, he learned to look past the whirlwind of heavenly activity that characterized Elijah's ministry. He looked past the ministry and saw the man. He was a good student, and he passed this final test at the end of his master's life. He saw the chariot of fire, he saw the whirlwind ascending to heaven, but he also saw the man. And because he saw the man, he got the mantle.

Lesson #29: If We Imitate Spiritual Fathers, They Will Lead Us to Christ

Lesson #30:

We Should Embrace God's Discipline, Knowing That It Has a Purpose and a Limit

Now some are puffed up, as though I were not coming to you. But I will come to you shortly, if the Lord wills, and I will know, not the word of those who are puffed up, but the power. For the kingdom of God is not in word but in power. What do you want? Shall I come to you with a rod, or in love and a spirit of gentleness?

1 Corinthians 4:18-21

Paul was able to discipline the church severely, as with a rod. He was just as able to comfort the church, as with a pillow and blanket. His letters leave the impression that he was able to switch back and forth between rod and pillow rather abruptly. This is because he was good at both comfort and discipline, and he recognized when and where each was needed.

The church today, as in every day, needs both the rod of discipline and the spirit of gentleness.

The rod is for within the church; it is not to be used on the rest of the world. Paul pointed this out a little later in the letter, in 1 Corinthians 5:12-13: *"For what have I to do with judging those also who are outside? Do you not judge those who are inside? But those who are outside God judges."*

Jesus' followers are called to hold themselves to a standard that is higher than any standard put upon them from the outside. The world usually does hold the church to high standards, and it should. It should expect the church look and act different from the rest of the world. Yet the standards that we impose upon ourselves should be even higher.

As we have previously seen (Lesson #17), there is a sense in which spiritual people cannot be judged by carnal people. But there is also a sense in which they can. Their outward behavior, their conduct in the world, is being watched and evaluated by nonbelievers, as it should be.

When the world looks to the church, it looks for power, not just words. It looks for otherworldly authority. It also looks for integrity and love.

One of the most common criticisms of the church by those outside is that it is full of hypocrisy. This accusation may be fair or unfair, depending on the circumstances. Nevertheless, it should be the goal of every Christian to make sure that the charge doesn't stick.

This does not mean that the church must be full of perfect people. It means that the church must exercise self-discipline.

The Corinthians were given a choice. They could discipline themselves or they could wait for Paul to do it. We likewise have the opportunity to discipline ourselves before we are disciplined by the Lord. We may not have an apostle threatening to come and straighten us out. Nevertheless, we know that God will make sure that we are disciplined one way or another.

It is much better to exercise self-discipline than to wait for God to do it. It is better still to discipline ourselves even as we ask the Father to discipline us. He is better at it and He knows what He is doing.

There is a passage in Isaiah (Isaiah 28:23-29) that describes how a farmer prepares the ground for sowing, breaking it up until it is soft. He plows the ground just as much as he needs to, and he knows ahead of time what the ground will look like when it is ready for the seed to be planted. In other words, he has a *purpose*.

Isaiah then describes what the farmer does to the crop after he has harvested it. He beats it with a stick! If you watched him without understanding his methods, you might think he was angry at the very wheat that he had worked so hard to grow. But again, he has a *purpose*. He beats it just hard enough and just long enough as he needs to, in order to separate it from the chaff.

The farmer's work may look violent to the untrained eye, but it is not senseless. It has a purpose. And because it has a purpose, it has a limit.

Listen to how Isaiah describes it:

"Give ear and hear my voice,
Listen and hear my speech.
Does the plowman keep plowing all day to sow?
Does he keep turning his soil and breaking the clods?
When he has leveled its surface,
Does he not sow the black cummin
And scatter the cummin,
Plant the wheat in rows,
The barley in the appointed place,
And the spelt in its place?
For He instructs him in right judgment,
His God teaches him.
For the black cummin is not threshed with a threshing sledge,
Nor is a cartwheel rolled over the cummin;
But the black cummin is beaten out with a stick,
And the cummin with a rod.
Bread flour must be ground;
Therefore he does not thresh it forever,
Break it with his cartwheel,
Or crush it with his horsemen.
This also comes from the Lord of hosts,
Who is wonderful in counsel and excellent in guidance."

Yes, the farmer threshes the wheat, but not forever. Yes, he beats the grain with a stick, but he doesn't run over it with a cartwheel or hit it with a hammer. That would be too much. The farmer doesn't do too much. He does enough.

Actually, it is possible that a farmer might, in his zeal, thresh the wheat a little bit harder or longer than necessary. He is, after all, only human.

God, on the other hand, is perfect in His discipline. When God disciplines us, it is for a specific purpose; therefore, it has a specific limit. It is the means to an end.

When He comforts us, however, it is not just the means to an end. God's comfort is an end in and of itself, and it has no limit.

Ephesians 2:7 tells us that God has saved us and made us alive in Christ for this purpose: *"...that in the ages to come He might show the exceeding riches of His grace in His kindness toward us in Christ Jesus."*

There is no limit to God's kindness toward us in Christ Jesus. He wants to take eternity to demonstrate this. It is for this wonderful and kind God that we strive to discipline ourselves in our own imperfect ways, and it is Him we ask to help us in His own perfect way.

Lesson #30: We Should Embrace God's Discipline, Knowing That It Has a Purpose and a Limit

Printed in Great Britain
by Amazon